So You're on the Ethics Committee?

A Primer and Practical Guidebook: 21st Century Practical Ethics Applied to 21st Century Health Care

By Richard E. Thompson, MD

American College of Physician Executives
4890 West Kennedy Boulevard, Suite 200
Tampa, Florida 33609-2575
813-287-2000 • www.acpe.org

ISBN: 0-9787306-0-7

Library of Congress Card Number: 2007924741

Printed in the United States of America by Lightning Sources, Inc., St. Louis, Missouri.

Contents

About the Author

Richard E. Thompson, MD (Washington U. School of Medicine, St. Louis, 1959), is a self-taught ethicist. For 12 years, he has read ethics with several mentors, chief among them his son, Paul B. Thompson, currently Distinguished Professor of Community, Agriculture, and Land Use Ethics at Michigan State University.

Dr. Thompson has taught ethics at the Ethics Institute, St. Petersburg College, St. Petersburg, FL, and Missouri State University, Springfield, MO. He is currently adjunct (online) instructor of Medical Ethics at Drury University in Springfield.

Dr. Thompson's column, *Ethical Aspects*, appears regularly in *Physician Executive* magazine. A collection of his *Ethical Aspects* columns is a companion CD to this primer and practical guidebook. Dr. Thompson is co-anchor of ACPE's online Ethics Forum.

Dr. Thompson has practiced pediatrics, been a pioneer neonatologist, and served as Vice President of the Illinois Hospital Association. For 20 years he was a writer, speaker, consultant and innovator in credentialing, physician performance evaluation, medical staff bylaws, and some areas of the Joint Commission's hospital standards.

The style of this *Ethics Committee Primer and Practical Guidebook* is similar to that of two of his other works, five editions of *The Medical Staff Leader's Practical Guidebook* (Opus, Marblehead, MA), and four editions of a practical manual on meeting JCAHO's medical staff standards, also published by Opus. Subsequent editions of these manuals are by other authors.

Dr. Thompson's other ACPE publications include *Keys to Winning Physician Support: Real Winners Don't Gag the Good Guys* (1999), *On Beyond Compliance* (2001), and a book that is unfortunately still timely, *Health Care Reform as Social Change* (1993).

Dr. Thompson lives in Springfield, MO, with his wife of 52 years, Joan, and the master of the house, Sebastian Tobias Thompson, an Affenpinscher (dog).

Please provide feedback about the usefulness of this primer and practical guidebook to Dr. Thompson (tmaret@sbcglobal.net), and suggest additional topics of interest for inclusion in the second edition.

Introduction

What This Book Is and Is Not

This book is for each member of the 21st Century hospital's ethics committee.

Ethics is an important consideration at the corporate office level, but that is not the subject of this book. The corporate office is far removed from day-to-day patient care, even if the corporate offices are in the same building as patient care units. In contrast, members of the hospital ethics committee are often right in the thick of current patient care activities.

This primer and practical guidebook is not an academically peer reviewed textbook. If your interest in 21st Century health care ethics is academic and philosophical in the metaphysical sense, then in addition to this primer you need a copy of Principles in *Biomedical Ethics: 5th Edition*, by Tom Beauchamp and James Childress (Oxford U. Press, New York and Oxford, 2001).

This primer really *is* a primer. That is: With apologies to readers who are students of ethics, the book provides a basic introduction for committee members who are not. Actually, even those well versed in ethics might learn something new in Chapters 1, 2, and 3. Properly applied, some of the differences between traditional metaphysical, philosophy-based schools of ethical thought and today's practical, applied ethics can make the expanded role of the ethics committee a little more understandable and a little less impossible to fulfill. The nature of that expanded role is indicated by categorization of today's health care issues as traditional medical ethics, organizational ethics applied to health care, and new issues in medical bioethics.

This primer and guidebook is not a substitute for your committee's own good judgment. Believe me, if it were possible to write an Answer Book in this difficult area, I would write it. However, there actually are no right answers in ethics. By definition, an ethical dilemma is a situation in which nothing that can be decided or done will be 100% right, in the sense of either correct or angelic, or 100% wrong, in the sense of either incorrect or evil.

Therefore, this book can only define and describe the expanded, tripartite field of health care ethics, provide beginning background information, help with committee methods and logistics, and suggest a few case scenarios to discuss for practice and further learning.

Indeed, at the bottom line, the ethics committee's usefulness and appropriateness depends on knowledge and understanding of your organization and the people in it, as much as on your ability to accurately apply ethical theories and principles and moral values.

This book is *not* about how to meet some federal or state requirement or Joint Commission standard. Hospitals have ethics committees for the best reason there is to have a committee, some would say the only good reason. That is, experience over the past few years confirms the value of ethics committee activities, from the viewpoint of practitioners who learn to rely upon this committee when ethical dilemmas are encountered.

Indeed, as in all areas of the survey, Joint Commission ethics and patients' rights standards now focus not on committee meetings, but on effective, patient-related activities of relevant and responsible individuals.

This primer and practical guidebook is not a book to put on the shelf. Keep it handy. Take it to each meeting of the ethics committee. Refer to it along with other relevant resources when designing suggested solutions to an ethics problem presented to the committee by a physician nurse, management team member, or patient and family member group.

Companion CD

On the companion CD to this book, you will find a collection of the author's *Ethical Aspects* columns, a regular feature in *Physician Executive* magazine. Using the book and CD together should enhance understanding of 21st Century health care ethics.

Part I

About Ethics

Chapter One

What Ethics Is and Is Not

How can we possibly avoid gridlock in the ethics committee if we skip the step of agreeing on the meaning of ethics and related words and phrases? The answer is, we cannot.

What is ethics, anyway?"

Ethics is many things to many people. To some, ethics is so obviously simple that we should just skip the step of agreeing on a destination and get started on the trip. The more people learn about ethics, the less inclined they are to dismiss ethics so lightly.

Ethics is a clumsy word, because it is singular but ends in s.

Ethics is about *how* people decide what they will and won't do. It is not about *why* people decide what they will and won't do. That is metaphysical philosophy.

Actually ethics is, academically, one of five branches of philosophy (metaphysics, epistemology, aesthetics, logic, and ethics). By the way, *ethics* and *logic* are first cousins. Indeed, without critical thinking skills and effective argumentation skills, ethics is like a computer with no operating system and no power cord. Guess who said that. I did. You think Aristotle had a computer?

Ethics is like an elephant. A definition and description of its trunk, its tusks, or its tail is accurate but incomplete.

To some, ethics and altruism are synonyms (they are not). Want to help the poor? Then don't give away all your money and join their ranks.

To a devoutly religious person, *ethics* and *religion* may be synonyms (they are not). Being religious is not a prerequisite to acting ethically.

The most common view of ethics may be that ethics is so ephemeral, ethereal, metaphysical, and idealistic that it should be left to pompous pontificating professional thinkers in a university's ivory towers. By the way, "pipe smoking" once fit beautifully into that alliteration but it doesn't anymore. Many of today's wise ethicists are women. And, try as some men and women will to totally equate the genders, few women ethicists smoke pipes.

What Ethics Is Not

Ethics is not legal compliance. Yet one of the most common mistakes made when discussing ethics is to conflate ethical reasoning with legal aspects of an issue. Does a Congressional Ethics Committee discuss, "Where is the justice, where is the integrity, in accepting bribes from special interests?" Or does it discuss, "How much of what kinds of bribes can we accept before doing something illegal?"

Indeed, ethical behavior and legal compliance behavior are diametrically opposed. Legal compliance is imposed from without, so compliance behavior is sidestepping regulations and going through the motions while continuing business as usual. Ethical behavior is motivated from within, so ethical behavior is to change when necessary if stakeholders' expressed needs are reasonable. (*Stakeholders* is a term used in ethics to indicate those who have an interest, a stake, in a decision and/or action of another person or group.)

In addition, ethically motivated people have vision. That is, they care about sustaining a business, a community, a planet over time, mindful of the needs of future generations.

Indeed, here is ethical reasoning in a nutshell: Include reasonable concerns of all stakeholders, and anticipate possible negative long-range consequences. I hasten to add, this is only part of the decision-making process, not the entire decision-making process. In the real world, the best business decisions can hardly ever be made on the basis of either economic reasoning or ethical reasoning alone.

At the bottom line, a company's operational ethic is determined by organizational leaders' understanding of the difference between legal compliance behavior and truly ethical behavior.

A hospital's operational ethic (no pun intended), determined by organizational leaders' collective viewpoints, is what happens after the doors to board rooms and executive offices close. Sometimes that is in marked contrast to the behavior suggested in the flowery language of much publicized Mission Statements and Codes of Ethics.

For example, ethical behavior requires the vision and honesty usually spoken of in the flowery posted promises. If one takes a long-range view, wanting to sustain a business over time, one is concerned about public trust and actually, honesty is the best policy. However, honesty has very little immediate economic value. If one's view is to ignore the future and be concerned only about maximizing this quarter's bottom line, then lying, cheating, and stealing are the best policies.

By the way, should that be a concern of the hospital's ethics committee, or is that none of the ethics committee's business? And conversely, should senior management be interested in the ethics committee's activities and signal to the organization that they are of high priority, or is ethics in the organization a thorn in the side of management, considered an obstruction to maximizing profit? Has your ethics committee discussed this matter? Should it?

See what I mean when I say that today's hospital ethics committees must decide anew the intended range and scope of its activities? That range and scope should be much broader and deeper than the traditional notion that a hospital ethics committee is concerned only with matters such as living wills and organ transplantation?

Continuing with *ethics is not…*

Ethics is not religion. Some people say they are going to present a logical ethical argument and then tell you about Jesus. Jesus certainly is one of the greatest virtue ethicists in the history of mankind. However, virtue ethics is not all there is to ethics. Furthermore, Jesus' followers sometimes seem to forget that Jesus was a wise self-educated man who may have traveled abroad, and who sounds like he may have gotten a few ideas from Aristotle.

Ethics is not morality anymore. True, you have probably learned somewhere that ethics and moral philosophy were synonyms in the olden days, and they still are in the academic community. Using the terms ethics and morals synonymously worked fine when the concept of morality was broad and deep.

Today, however, thanks to modern-day moralists whose narrow view of morality is a list of thou shalt nots focused primarily on sexual behavior, marital relationships, and reproductive biology, ethics and morality are no longer synonymous.

In addition, the modern-day moralist's world view is negative and punitive. In contrast, to the ethicist, a life well-lived (following the human instincts of a love of learning and a desire to live in a civilized society, can be a self-fulfilled life, happy, in the Aristotelian sense, even though human nature dictates that no one is perfect.

Ironically, we may owe the emergence of narrow morality a vote of thanks for an important insight. That is: *ethical reasoning* and *moral values* never were actually synonymous! Application of ethical principles is an intellectual exercise. In contrast, one's moral values are beliefs, usually based more on emotion than logic. Genuine moral intelligence is a combination of intellect and controlled emotion.

Example: Economic wisdom suggests closing a money-losing hospital service. Ethical reasoning informs us that there is a valid utilitarian argument for doing so. That is, money saved can perhaps benefit a greater number of patients. However, if the money-losing service is the high-risk newborn nursery then morality may require that we find some other way to save money.

What would really seem unethical would be to close the newborn service, ignore patient needs in other areas, and use money formerly spent on sick newborns to enhance personal incomes of shareholders and the CEO. Is this argument logical? Not completely, because its beginning assumption is a set of moral values. That is: (1) I am a former neonatologist with strong feelings in this area, and (2) I am concerned (an emotion) about health care costs related to the competitive, profit-taking model of health care.

For many, awareness of ethics begins with learning to recognize the difference between what we think and how we feel.

Ethics at first glance seems simple. Ethics is not simple at all. However, neither is ethics a secret society whose members are the only ones capable of understanding ethics and applying it usefully to life's everyday difficult situations.

At the bottom line, then, let's say again for emphasis. The best way to choose civilized behaviors is an eclectic mix of ethical reasoning (critical thinking, intellectual effort) and heartfelt, emotionally based moral values (compassion, trustworthiness, conscientiousness, etc.).

Finally, contrary to what you may have been brought up to believe, ethical behavior is not necessarily a sacrifice. Indeed, perhaps the best reason to act ethically is to serve one's own reasonable self-interests and to pursue happiness for oneself! Be careful, though. There is a difference between reasonable self-interest and selfishness, and we're talking about Aristotle's definition of happiness.

What is the difference between reasonable self-interest and selfishness? Aristotle explains: "The love of self is a feeling implanted by nature, but selfishness is rightly censured, because selfishness is not mere love of self, but the love of self in excess, like the miser's love of money."[1]

What is Aristotle's definition of happiness? Aristotle wrote that everything has a purpose. The sail of a ship enables the ship to move. A hammer drives a nail. Humans have two unique purposes, argued Aristotle. One is to learn and exhibit intelligence. The other is to know the difference between moral and immoral behavior, in the broadest sense, and to choose to act morally so that society remains civilized. When a man lives according to that guideline, argued Aristotle, he can achieve the highest level of happiness and self-satisfaction.

Ethics in a Nutshell

For practical everyday purposes, ethics is simpler than a lot of people make it sound.

Ethics is:

- Awareness and display of some virtues (such as justice, courage, wisdom, temperance/moderation, caring, frugality, industry).
- A sense of responsibility/duty/morality, including awareness of beneficence and non-maleficence as desirable consequences (results) of one's thoughts and actions.
- Respect for the rights of self and others (such rights as autonomy/self-determination, dignity, privacy, ownership of property).
- A sense of social and economic justice.
- Taking a long range view (vision).
- Pausing to think! This might be the hardest part of being ethical, because almost everything in today's society informs us that speed is a common good much to be desired.

References

1. Aristotle. *Politics*, Book II (translated by B. Jowett), introduction by H.W.C. Davis. Oxford, England: Clarendon Press, 1905, pp. 62-63.

Chapter 2

Theoretical Ethics

The story of Western ethics usually starts with Aristotle, who lived in Athens, Greece, around 500 B.C. Eastern philosophies and religions, such as Buddhism, Confucianism, and Taoism, were beginning to develop at about the same time.

Aristotle was a student of Plato who was a student of Socrates. Aristotle's idea was that ethical living was a result of personal qualities called virtues. Aristotle's four virtues are:

- **Prudence.** The difference between knowledge and prudence (wisdom) is understanding.
- **Courage.** Willingness to take a risk, in this context for the purpose of helping another person.
- **Temperance** (Moderation). You have probably heard the saying, "All things in moderation." Here is an example of what Aristotle means by moderation. If one saves a person from drowning, one exhibits the virtue, courage. Too little courage is cowardice. However, if one jumps in to save a drowning person when one cannot swim, that is no longer courage; that is foolhardiness.

  In an Age of Extremism, rediscovery of Aristotelian moderation might be the most important ethical quest, because it reflects nature. To put this point another way, there is a very narrow physiologic range…a range of moderation…in which we can survive. If our body pH is off by a few tenths of a point either way, we are dead. If our body temperature is above 107°F we are dead; if it is below 90 we are dead. Why should we be surprised that moderation, one of nature's most observable characteristics, should lead us to make the best decisions when the goal is to keep society civilized?
- **Justice.** Think fairness. In health care, questions of economic and distributive justice are important themes in political debates about what U.S. health care policy should look like.

It is hard to imagine an ethical life not grounded to some degree in Aristotelian virtues. Being virtuous is not all there is to ethics, however. Even beginning ethics students can drop the names of a few well-known schools of ethical thought, and the names of famous professional thinkers associated with them. Here are five examples.

Virtue Ethics

See above. Aristotle was the first great Western virtue ethicist. Other virtue ethicists with whom you are acquainted include Yeshua (Jesus of Nazareth) and Benjamin Franklin. For another example of virtue ethics, read the Boy Scout oath. Indeed, virtue ethics is the form of ethics with which many people are most familiar. Virtue, or at least lip service to virtue, is everywhere.

Utilitarianism

Jeremy Bentham and John Stuart Mill taught that one's actions should result in the greatest possible net happiness. By definition, using this approach, everyone is not going to end up happy, in the sense of pleased, benefited by the results of a decision and/or action. By the way, one basic flaw in this theory, if it is left to stand alone, is the need to agree on a definition of happiness.

Because utilitarians focus on consequences, meaning results both good and bad, utilitarianism is an example of a consequentialist ethical theory. Virtue ethics, in contrast, is a non-consequentialist theory; do what is right regardless of the consequences.

Can one truly ignore either virtue or results? Is it becoming clear that no ethical theory, if left to stand alone, if applied absolutely, is free from flaws? Is it becoming clear that today's ethicists are justified in abandoning the focus on schools of thought to focus instead on common objective, time-proven principles contained in each school of ethical thought that has survived centuries of testing and criticism?

Deontology/Duty Based Ethics/Kantianism

Immanuel Kant, whom some believe to be the greatest Western philosopher since the Big Three in ancient Athens (Socrates, Plato, and Aristotle), taught that ethical choices must be based on absolute rules (categorical imperatives), plus having the will to follow the rules.

Furthermore, Kant believed that ethical actions must put the human worth of every individual first. Like Aristotelian virtue, Kantian duty/obligation is familiar to us all still today as a time-proven objective (not absolute, but objective) basis for a society's common morality.

Rights-Based Ethics

John Locke taught that ethical behavior takes root in respect for certain inalienable God-given rights, such as life, liberty, and ownership of property. Sound familiar? If so, that is because Thomas Jefferson borrowed Locke's construct in writing the Declaration of Independence—"life, liberty, and the pursuit of happiness." Ironically, Locke was an Englishman.

Locke's natural rights ethical philosophy is the basis of modern day human rights ethics, and his work is also the basis of much in English law, the system of law in the United States except for the state of Louisiana where the legal system is a mixture of English and French jurisprudence. It was Locke, for example, who suggested that the punishment must fit the crime.

Note, by the way, that traditional ethicists often ended up talking and writing about political philosophy and ethics in addition to ethics as a personal belief system. One of Aristotle's major works is *The Nichomachean Ethic*, a long treatise on personal virtues. Aristotle's father's name was Nichomacheaus, and so was his son's. At about the same time, Aristotle produced another major work on political philosophy and ethics. Thus, since the beginning of Western ethics, the influence of personal ethics on politics, and vice versa, has been well recognized and much described.

Today, rights-based ethics is seen in many situations, not always with good results. Indeed, in today's society, the meaning and application of rights-based ethics has changed. The original idea was to be mindful of the rights of others. In today's self-centered world, the idea is protection of one's own rights. The result is not the pursuit of happiness for everyone, but rather one legal contest after another. And what about Locke's original notion that respecting ownership of property makes for a more civilized society? In this Age of Extreme Rights, identity theft is a major problem. Does that sound like a society in which ownership of property is honored and respected?

Today, even groups that have benefited most from the "I Have A Right…!" age urge moving on beyond stubbornly defended positions to a cooperative effort to apply ethical principles such as integrity, truth telling, and social and economic justice.

Indeed, legal contests to decide which person's or group's rights are to prevail result in limited gains for some, and total losses for others. Mutual application of a few time-tested ethical principles might result in less gain for some, but allow most participants to improve their positions in some way. At least, that is the original and lasting notion called ethics.

Divine Command

For some people, doing the right thing is simple. As a popular bumper sticker proclaims, "God spoke it; I believe it; that settles it." This fatalistic divine command approach is different from the idea of our forefathers who grounded government in the idea of divine guidance.

In some hospitals, each person and group, including the ethics committee, is bound to abide by religious rules and directives. Each new ethics committee member must be oriented to these rules, preferably in a one-on-one session so there is ample opportunity for questions and answers. This orientation should, in most instances, be conducted by the committee chair or his/her designee *and* a member of the clergy or his/her designee. The people orienting the new board member must themselves be thoroughly conversant with the religious rules and directives relevant to health care. These directives are, in one way, laws with which the committee must comply. In another sense, however, they are the ethics of the religious group that owns the hospital set down in clear, although not always concise, written form.

Continuing education sessions of the committee must include reminders and re-orientation regarding relevant religious rules. Deliberations of ethics committees in hospitals owned by religious groups—protestant or Catholic or otherwise—must observe these religious directives.

Except in hospitals where religious rules convert ethical reasoning into a form of legal compliance, ethics committees may find the principalism approach described in the next chapter more useful than traditional ethical theory constructs when the committee engages in ethical reasoning.

Chapter 3

21st Century Practical Ethics Applied:
Principalism, and How to Recognize an Ethical Dilemma

In the past, people picked one ethical school of thought and tried to make it fit every difficult situation (ethical dilemma). Once a utilitarian, always a utilitarian. Or one allowed the virtue of compassion always to overrule the reality of economic and political feasibility.

This approach to ethics, trying to fit every foot into the same size shoe, not only produced some less than wise decisions and actions, it also produced great guilt feelings, because the goal was serving a set of rules rather than serving the greater good.

The traditional purist approach to ethics eventually fell into disrepute, because no ethical theory left to stand alone is free from flaws. Because every ethical theory is flawed and thus cannot stand up to all the "Yes, but, what if..." questions, and because I am forced to pick just one (went the thinking), why not just give up ethics altogether?

That's a hard argument to refute. So people did abandon ethical principles, replacing them with the notion of subjectivism.

The Outback Steakhouse motto captures the essence of subjectivism. "No Rules, Just Right." A subjectivist makes no attempt to frame and follow guidelines for living. Live only in the moment.

How well does this work? The shortest way to answer this question is to suggest: Go to an Outback Steakhouse and have a nice dinner and, if you are not a teetotaler, a couple of good drinks. Then, start a fight at the bar. Then attempt to leave without paying. Are there truly no rules?

Subjectivism remains popular, however, because it is a really good form of rationalization, in the sense of artificial justification for what we really want to do. For example, since "Always tell the truth" doesn't work, why not get comfortable with lying to or at least misleading people? We might actually recognize that the problem is not, "tell the truth;" the problem is "always." But who wants to go there, because then we would have to admit that while "tell the truth" does not work as an absolute principle, it certainly has withstood the test of time as an objective principle, to be observed unless at some point another ethical principle in a situation—a greater truth—trumps truth telling.

Still think ethics is simple? Hang in there.

The bottom line: Subjectivism is not a viable alternative to compulsive use of ethical theories. If society is to be at all civilized, there must be rules and guidelines. The alternative would be anarchy and chaos. No rules is not an option.

Pure philosophical theoretical ethics and subjectivism are opposite extremes. Surely, if Aristotle's moderation principle works, somewhere in the middle there is a better way. There is, and modern day ethicists have found it.

In recent years, many ethicists stopped focusing on differences between various ethical theories and started looking for similarities. Lo and behold, what emerged is the insight that several objective but not absolute ethical principles are found in many if not most traditional ethical theories.

That led to the conclusion that the most useful, practical school of ethical thought is probably an eclectic synthesis of several objective but not absolute principles that have withstood the test of time, and without which no traditional school of ethical thought seems complete. Thus, ethicists now make their tools, ethical principles, fit the job, instead of trying to make every job fit whatever is in their toolbox (an absolute ethical theory).

The Difference between "Practical Ethics Applied" and Subjectivism

Some people call the modern-day principles-based approach practical ethics applied. Professional thinkers who must reduce everything to -isms call this practical approach principalism. By the way, note that time spent naming and categorizing ideas is worthwhile, because otherwise there would be no clear way of sharing and discussing ideas.

Some accuse principalists of coming around to subjectivism by the back door. Isn't this just a self-satisfying but self-deceiving intellectual exercise? No, it is not. Well, actually, it can be if the following key idea is not incorporated into the principalist's thinking.

Today's practical, principles-based ethicists do state firm guidelines and principles: "Tell the truth." However, note that they drop the word "always." That is, in applying time-tested principles, a modern-day ethicist who is both a good thinker and morally honest understands and uses the difference between an objective principle and an absolute principle. "Honey, how do you like my new hairdo?" What good is served by always telling the absolute truth in that situation? Is there not a greater good to be served than compulsive adherence to truth telling?

If you are interested in learning more about ethics, look up the prima facie concept of Ross. On the face of it, truth telling will be the first choice in an ethical dilemma. However, look beyond the face of the situation and other factors might dictate otherwise. Truth telling and other objective, time-tested ethical values are most useful if considered as prima facie values, not as absolute values, categorical imperatives that must always be served.

An example used in university ethics classes is: Suppose it is World War II time and Anne Frank is hiding in your attic. When Nazi soldiers come to the door to find and kill her, would you say, "She's right up there, the stairway on your right?" Most people would not, and not for purely political reasons such as hatred of the Nazi party.

We refuse to betray Anne Frank even though we strive to be truthful and are very reluctant to deceive. Why? Because in this situation, as in most true dilemmas, there are two truths and both cannot be equally served. The Kantian principle of respecting human worth trumps the ethical principle of telling the truth.

Note that this example demonstrates a basic flaw in unrevised Kantianism. Often, the impossibility of strictly adhering to this code can create frustration in a person who truly wants to be ethically motivated.

Keep in mind, as you deliberate in committee, that in most health care situations with ethical aspects, there is a greater truth and a lesser truth. If you want to be a principalist rather than a subjectivist, strive to honor the greater truth in any given situation.

For example: Should doctors tell the truth? Yes, but not absolutely. For years I honored a request from Cousin Earl and his wife, Margaret, to keep from the rest of the family the fact that Margaret had cancer. To you that must seem an eccentric if not crazed request and I thought so too, but I withheld that judgment. No one can truly be an ethicist until he or she learns the art and skill of accepting without approving. Had you known Earl and Margaret, I believe you would have recognized some greater truths that made my decision the right one.

In principalist ethics, by the way, there is no need to choose whether one is "non-consequentialist" or "consequentialist." The "right thing to do" must not only mean high-minded; it must also mean correct. That is, one must try to accurately predict the outcome of one's decisions and actions. (Two weeks before she died, Margaret wrote a letter to her family that said in part, "I believe it is time to advise you of my condition...." Earl later wrote a book about their 17-year journey. They both died at peace. As you can tell, I continue to live with my decision.

That is the nature of life's difficult situations, life's ethical dilemmas.

How to Recognize a Difficult Situation (Ethical Dilemma)

An ethical dilemma has three characteristics:

1. One's actions and decisions affect other stakeholders in the situation.
2. The impact is long-lasting.
3. Nothing one can decide to do will be either 100% right (angelic, correct) or 100% wrong (evil, incorrect)

Here Is Where We Are Now

In the first part of this book we are populating our ethicist's toolbox. We now have a beginning set of ethical theories and a blueprint, principalism with moral underpinnings. If we were computers, this would be our software. Next we will add to out tool kit the equivalent of a computer's operating system, the skills of critical thinking and persuasive argumentation.

Part II

How to Think and Argue Like an Ethicist

Chapter 4

Critical Thinking (Uncommon Sense)

> *"Oh, I knew there'd be hell to pay,*
> *But I thought o' that a little too late.*
> *I know what I was feelin'*
> *But what was I thinkin'?"*
> — Dierks Bentley

Critical thinking, which I like to call uncommon sense, is informed, reasoned, responsible human thought about an idea, an event, or a person. Feelings, emotions, come naturally. There is nothing natural about critical thinking. It is a skill that must be learned and practiced.

Good judgment is the result of good critical thinking. Bad judgment is often the result of acting on feelings such as the sex urge, anger, or pride, without stopping to listen to reason.

Critical thinking differs from skepticism. A skeptic has a predisposition not to believe. In contrast, good critical thinkers have an open mind. That is, they are willing to accept new discoveries that result from the critical thinking process. Good critical thinkers are not simply looking for ways to validate some preconceived notion.

Common sense and conventional wisdom are what people believe without stopping to think. Common sense and conventional wisdom sometimes serve us well, but often they mislead us.

Sometimes common sense and conventional wisdom are products of a bandwagon psychology that perpetuates a mistaken assumption or faulty conclusion. "Are you sure what you are saying makes sense?" "Yes, because everybody I've talked to says the same thing."

Other times, common sense and conventional wisdom betray us when we try to transfer them from one situation to the next. In a football game, a player catches a pass in the end zone. The play is ruled a touchdown and the pass-catching player's team is awarded six points. Later in the game, another player on the same team catches a pass in the end zone. Common sense suggests that this is a touchdown, too. But it isn't. The second player is an interior lineman, an "ineligible receiver," so the play is illegal and the pass-catching team is penalized.

Like everyone else, good critical thinkers ask questions. But unlike everyone else, good critical thinkers listen to and evaluate the answers. If an answer is unacceptable or incomplete, the critical thinker asks follow-up questions.

Traveling Salesman to Old New England Whaler: How did you lose your leg?

Old Whaler: It got bit off.

Traveling Salesman (not a good critical thinker): Oh, I see.

Some Elements of Critical Thinking

Ask Sharp Questions

Critical thinkers accept very little at face value. Hercule Poirot, Sherlock Holmes, the detectives on *Law and Order*, and the *CSI* investigators do not accept an explanation unless every fact in evidence fits the explanation. They continually ask, "Why?" Critical thinkers are always looking for clues. He doesn't have a clue means, "He is not a good thinker."

Be Well-Informed

Critical thinking must be informed. The less we know the easier we are to fool. At a football game, what would you say if someone tells you to jump up and yell "Block that kick!" when one team or the other punts? When one team or other tries a field goal? When one team or other kicks off?

If An Answer Exists, Look It Up

Will: What is the population of Chicago?

Donna: It seems to me it's about half a million.

Will: Naw, can't be. Must be closer to a million by now.

Donna: Well, Harry's from Chicago and he said once that the city's too big, that's all I know."

Expressing opinions about facts is a waste of time. Furthermore, opinions sometimes are re-told as facts. Misinformation spreads that way. "Joe, Will says there are a million people in Chicago now." "Is that a fact? Then Shirley is wrong. I'll tell her."

Do you think Donna and Will have computers? Do you think Donna and Will know how to look up the population of Chicago? (Both are far astray of the fact).

Don't Oppose An Idea You Agree With

Many times, two people start arguing, the argument turns into a quarrel, and then it turns out the two people did not really disagree. After the two have apologized to each other, they ask each other questions and find out they were talking about two different things and didn't know it.

When two people take time to be sure they are on the same page, quarrels don't break out as often. If you find yourself disagreeing with someone, put your hands in the air in a "time out" sign and say, "Whoa, just a minute." Ask, "What do you mean by that?" or "What exactly are you talking about?" or "Can you give me an example?"

Beware of Two or More Questions in One

"Should I go to college to learn philosophy, if so where, and should I join a sorority?" My grammar and syntax checker does not like that sentence. No wonder. That is a terrible question, because it is actually four questions in one. Much misunderstanding can be avoided by separating a complex question into several separate questions. Should I go to college? If I decide "yes," is that because I want to study philosophy? Which college shall I go to? Should I join a sorority?

The technique of dividing the question is well known to people who chair meetings of any kind of group. The chairperson of the homeowners' association does not ask the board, "Shall we have a Fourth of July picnic again this year, at City Park, catered by Brown's Restaurant, on the Saturday closest to the fourth beginning at noon and charge people five dollars to attend?"

Polltakers and questionnaires often frame two questions in one. "Will you be voting for the Democratic candidate because you want the country to be free and prosperous?" Advertisers are good at this, too. Sometimes sharp advertisers use the "two questions in one" technique to limit our response choices. "Do you think this beer is less filling or do you think it tastes great?"

Learn and Practice Idea Algebra

Algebra is the mathematical skill of turning an unknown into a known by balancing two sides of an equation.

$2X + 4 = 20$

The equal sign makes that statement an equation. The question is, what number is X? To solve that equation, one must keep it balanced. That is, we must not do anything to one side of the equation that we do not do to the other side of the equation.

2X + 4 minus 4 = 20 minus 4.
2X = 16
2X divided by 2 = 16 divided by 2
X = 8

Idea algebra is the skill of keeping ideas balanced by not doing anything to one side of an idea that we do not do to the other side of an idea.

For example: Before the 2004 presidential election, incumbent vice president Richard Cheney urged voters not to have "political amnesia." That is, Vice President Cheney urged voters to remember past actions of Senators John Kerry and John Edwards, asking voters to agree with him that the two senators had made a lot of mistakes in the past. Voters practicing uncommon sense (if they thought the suggestion a good one) applied the suggestion to Vice President Cheney and President Bush as well.

Another use of idea algebra is looking for relationships between two ideas or observations. If there is a right femoral artery, we should expect a left femoral artery; otherwise anatomists would just say, "This is the femoral artery." Idea algebra is very important in ethical reasoning. "If there is value in truth, what is there in falsehood?"
(Trust and truth are ideas that do not exist in a vacuum. They are related. Where one is missing, so is the other.

Beware Claims Based on Statistics

Science is so respected that if one presents a claim as though it were a scientific fact, the claim is more likely to be believed. To avoid being fooled by statistics, ask good questions and look for relationships between two or more statistics.

"I know the average depth of this river is only three feet, but before I go swimming tell me, how deep is the river right here?"

Hospital A claims in advertising: "Our hospital is safe because the mortality rate from heart attack is only 4 percent." How can we know whether or not to believe that claim?

First, keep in mind that no hospital can really keep you safe from dying. In spite of medical miracles, the death rate in the United States is the same as it has always been. It is one apiece. Next, ask Hospital A's Performance Improvement (Quality Assurance) Department for a couple of related statistics. "What percentage of the time is your diagnosis of heart attack correct?" and "What percentage of heart attack patients do you refer to another hospital?" If Hospital A diagnoses heart attacks correctly only 60 percent of the time, some patients treated for heart attack never really had a heart attack. If Hospital B correctly diagnoses heart attack 98 percent of the time, plus Hospital A transfers its sickest patients to Hospital B, then even if Hospital B's heart attack mortality rate is 8%, Hospital B might be a safer place for a patient who really has a heart attack.

In politics and business, it is important always to ask, "What statistic are they *not* telling me about?" "The employment rate is up so you should re-elect me." What is happening to related statistics, such as the percentage of part-time jobs, temporary jobs, and jobs without benefits such as health care?

Chapter 5

Argumentation Skills:
It's Green So It's a Frog; Trust Me on That
Ethical Reasoning and Socratic Dialogue/Debate

Argumentation skills are another essential tool in the ethicist's tool box. Ethical reasoning and critical thinking are used in calm exchanges of ideas known as Socratic dialogue/debate. This process is a form of argument.

Argue and *quarrel* are not synonyms. A quarrel is a bitter exchange of angry insults and threats between two enemies. Nobody wins a quarrel, in the sense of being able to influence another's thinking. In contrast, an argument is a calm and reasonable exchange of ideas. In an argument, everyone ordinarily wins in the sense that the thinking of all participants is usually sharpened and clarified.

An argument is two or more assumptions related in some way to arrive at a conclusion. If the assumptions are incorrect, or if the suggested relationship between two facts, observations, or ideas does not indeed exist, then the argument is flawed.

Like critical thinking, argumentation (rhetoric, in the positive academic sense) is the subject of entire books and of many university courses.

"It's green so it's a frog" is an argument.

Assumptions

It is green.
Frogs are green.

Conclusion

Therefore, it is a frog.

How do we recognize that "It's green so it's a frog" is a flawed argument? First, we know better. A blade of grass is not a frog and neither is a dollar bill. Thus, our informed knowledge base allows us to think critically (use uncommon sense) and reject the flawed argument.

But what if someone uses this kind of argument to convince us to see things his or her way, and we don't know much about the subject under discussion? If the argument is something we want to believe, we will probably be fooled unless we critically examine the structure of the argument.

The frog argument has three building blocks.

A = it
B = green
C = frog

The structure of the argument is:

A = B
C = B
A = C.

An argument built that way is usually flawed. Two things that have a common characteristic are not necessarily identical to each other.

(A) Country music songs are (B) built using an 8-note scale and accidentals.
(C) Piano concertos are (B) built using an 8-note scale and accidentals.
(A) Country music songs are (B) piano concertos.

In contrast, the structure of a valid argument is:

A = B
B = C
A = C

This (A) is a computer (B).
Computers (B) are machines (C).
Therefore, this (A) is a machine (C).

Ah, in this argument there is a clear connection between (A) and (C). This argument is correctly structured and therefore is a valid argument, if the two assumptions are correct and the relationship between the two truly exists. Again, note how important an adequate knowledge base is to making and identifying valid arguments.

Keep in mind that even if an argument is correctly structured, the argument is flawed if one or more of the assumptions is incorrect or misleading.

All apples are fruit.
All fruit are citrus.
All apples are citrus.

Can you spot the flaw in that argument? (All fruit are not citrus).

Question assumptions before accepting conclusions. Also, always ask yourself, "What is this person trying to get me to believe?"

Right now, what am I trying to get you to believe about effective argumentation skills? Am I presenting information or am I presenting an argument? Or am I presenting a little of both? Do you have any questions yet? If so, discuss them in an educational session of the ethics committee. If not, go back and read the chapter on Critical Thinking.

Ethical Reasoning

Ethical reasoning is a special application of effective argumentation.

Truth-telling breeds trust.	A = B
Trust is a common good.	B = C
Truth-telling is a common good	A = C

All ethical/moral arguments are weak, because usually one of the assumptions is controversial, or at least debatable.

Informal Arguments

The examples above are syllogisms. Syllogisms, invented by Aristotle, are formal arguments. Most arguments are informal. One must really search between the lines to find the starting assumptions of most arguments. Also, one must derive relationships between assumptions that a speaker or writer intends, rather than depending on a clear statement of assumptions and relationships.

In everyday conversation, and in listening to, reading, or watching political speeches, ads and commercials, and news commentators, the most important, most often-used argumentation skill is awareness of *fallacies*. The ability to spot fallacies in others' arguments and avoid them in one's own arguments makes one hard to fool and at the same time an effective voice in the world of ideas. More about that in the next chapter.

Chapter 6

The Fallacies

The most common, easily recognizable flaw in an argument is a statement that masquerades as an appeal to reason (critical thinking) but that is really an appeal to some strong emotion such as anger, pride, fear, patriotism, or hatred. Such an appeal to emotion instead of reason is called a fallacy.

Fallacies may be introduced into an argument accidentally when people do not think carefully enough about the difference between *I think* and *I feel.* However, professional propagandists are skilled at purposely using fallacies to deceive or mislead us. In health care ethics, fallacies are common for both reasons.

Frequently refer to the following sample list of common fallacies. Become aware of fallacies in the arguments of others. Avoid inadvertent insertion of a fallacy into one of your own arguments. Of course if you are purposely using a fallacy to deceive and mislead someone, that's different. Machiavelli would be proud of you.

Also, if you want to have some fun, keep a copy of the following list by your TV set. Practice spotting fallacies in advertisements, newscasts, political speeches, and prime time dramas and comedies. The beautiful woman standing by the auto in a TV commercial is a red herring fallacy, attempting to distract us from matters such as frequency of repair and resale value. Good heavens, who would buy a car simply because there is a beautiful woman standing by it? On second thought, see how effective the purposeful use of fallacies can be?

Some Fallacies

Argument to the People

This is mass psychology, an appeal to public emotion, a suggestion of what "the American people" want. For example, disagreement might be equated with opposition to traditional values. "Anyone who doesn't vote for the Democrats is against God, country, motherhood, and apple pie."

Questionable Claim

Either the truth is exaggerated and embellished, or the claim is an outright lie. "I did not have sex with that woman."

Some questionable claims are nonmaleficent; that is, they do no harm. Indeed, in advertising we expect outright lies but harmless ones that often amuse us. "World's Biggest Hamburger!"

However, in health care ethics, there is nothing funny about relying upon a questionable claim because in health care the stakes are extremely high. "There is absolutely no way to stay within budget except to cut the quality of the services we provide."

Vagueness

The meaning is not clear. "The shooting of the hunters was terrible." Are the hunters poor marksmen, or was there an awful hunting accident? "Jordan always beats his Grandpa at golf, which pleases him." Pleases whom? Grandpa or Jordan?

Inconsistency (Doublespeak)

Different folks get different strokes. One day a political candidate tells a convention of condominium developers that strengthening the economy is his highest priority. The next day he tells a convention of environmentalists that preserving natural resources is his highest priority.

Believing Two or More Conflicting Things at Once (Doublethink)

Two or more ideas or happenings are incompatible, but we believe that they can coexist. "Sure, all my credit cards are maxed out and I have a low bank balance and payday isn't for two weeks yet, but I'm sure we can afford to buy us both new golf clubs, new running shoes, and the boat."

Ad Hominem Abusive

This is an attempt to defeat an argument by discrediting the person making the argument. Think insult. Today's campaign ads are almost entirely *ad hominem* abusives. When such personal attacks are used, a reasoned argument usually disintegrates into an angry quarrel. "Her ideas are no good because she cheats on her husband." "You wouldn't re-elect him would you? You do know, don't you, that he drank a lot in college." Note use of the third person in the examples. People often deliver an *ad hominem* abusive behind the person's back. Unfortunately, people experienced at working in an organizational setting are all too familiar with *ad hominem* abusives used as a vicious weapon.

In health care ethics, many issues are highly emotional. One task of the Ethics Committee is to keep discussion of highly charged issues on a calm, productive level, which is only possible if reasoned arguments are not allowed to deteriorate into alley fights.

Ad Hominem Circumstantial

This is an attempt to defeat an argument by placing the person in a group, then attacking the group. The implication is that the person's argument is defeated not on its merits, but by discrediting a group of people that might say such a thing. "That's exactly what I would expect a doctor to say." Or (with a sneer), "He's a liberal."

Red Herring (Distraction)

This is also known as changing the subject. "I understand you would like me to get a better job, honey, but I'm really worried about you. Have you told Dr. Brown that you haven't been sleeping well lately?"

"It is all right that seniors don't have enough money to buy the high priced prescriptions they need, because driving on the highway is dangerous, too."

Straw Man (a Setup)

A new assumption is introduced into the conversation, then defended. "I know my new golf clubs cost a lot but exercise is good for the heart and you don't want me to have a heart attack, do you?"

Provincialism

The facts are less important than allegiance to an idea or group. At a football game, the referee calls, "Offside." Everybody on this side of the stadium believes the referee is right; everybody on that side believes he is wrong.

Is/Ought Fallacy

This is the belief that tradition is always best. "There's no need to discuss it any further, because this is the way it is now and has been for years and things ought to stay the same."

Slippery Slope

This is an attempt to defeat an opposing argument by suggesting harm sometime in the future. "If euthanasia is legalized, what will happen next is exactly what happened in Nazi Germany when Hitler tried to cleanse the Aryan race by killing all the Jews."

"Give her an inch, and she'll take a mile."

In health care ethics—actually, in all applications of ethics— there is a fine line between a distracting, unsubstantiated slippery slope argument and a carefully thought out evaluation of possible future adverse happenings.

Either/Or Fallacy

This is falsely assuming that there are only two possible choices, then picking one choice and defending it, as opposed to brainstorming to come up with several alternative choices. Either/Or behavior is position taking and results in gridlock. Brainstorming behavior is problem-solving and can lead to the discovery of overlooked solutions.

"The only choices are to ignore and allow exploitative profit-taking invited by the managed care system, or socialized medicine. You don't want socialized medicine, do you?"

Please keep in mind: This list of fallacies and examples of each are provided for the purpose of introducing you to fallacies. Getting bogged down in discussing and deciding whether a fallacy is a red herring or a straw man is counterproductive, a true waste of time. The point is to be aware of and learn to recognize various kinds of appeals to emotion disguised as appeals to critical thinking, and to strengthen our own arguments by keeping them as fallacy free as possible.

Also, we have noted that the context here is ethical reasoning. If this were a primer and practical guidebook on polemics (political persuasion), avoiding appeals to emotion is the last thing you want to do.

That is one reason, by the way, that it is critically important to be aware of and recognize the difference between an ethical argument and a political argument. It is fair to fool people with fallacies in politics, but don't fool people with fallacies in ethics committee discussions. That wouldn't be ethical.

Part III

About Health Care Ethics

Chapter 7

The Three Faces of 21st Century Health Care Ethics

Until recent years, hospital ethics committees were one-dimensional. That is, ethics committees primarily pursued activities designed to help practitioners, patients, and family members deal with dilemmas that arise in the context of caring for hospitalized patients.

Examples include but are not limited to informed consent, confidentiality of personal medical information, care of the irreversibly ill and the elderly (living wills, hospice), organ transplantation, safety of human research subjects, and purposeful interruption of a pregnancy.

In passing, note that "purposeful interruption of a pregnancy" is an attempt to keep discussion and debate of a sensitive situation calm and reasonable. Let us argue, not quarrel. Such attempts at calmer language, avoiding red flag trigger words, are of course criticized and loudly rejected by extreme position takers. "Why disguise murder and killing by using softer words??!!?"

Today, a major part of the ethics committee's agenda continues to relate to the medical ethics issues listed above.

However, the activities and helpfulness of a fully developed 21st Century ethics committee should now be expanded to reflect the three faces of 21st Century health care ethics, which in turn reflect the expanded realities of 21st Century health care.

The following categorization is purely arbitrary, simply an attempt to help us organize our thinking and no more than that.

The three faces of modern day health care ethics are:

Traditional Medical Ethics

Some things never change. The issues listed above remain immensely important to the stakeholders involved in these dilemmas. By the way, we must not assume familiarity with these issues just because the words are familiar. Many of these issues continually present us with new dilemmas. For example, living wills are now a welcome and well-accepted relief from the illusion that there are no fates worse than death. Should euthanasia of the self-determination type be added to hospice and palliative care as alternatives offered to the irreversibly ill and elderly?

That is no longer an academic, rhetorical question. Serious proposals to legalize euthanasia so that the reality of assisted self-determination can be better regulated require that we face up to this issue, do they not?

Organizational Ethics Applied to Health Care

The unique nature of the hospital business makes awareness of ethical aspects of business decisions extremely important. "Health care institutions are, in fact, business organizations, with most of the problems faced by corporate management in other fields. They differ, however, in that health care holds a special place among human needs."[1]

Examples of organizational issues with important ethical aspects include: The definition of reasonable profit, the related issue of arbitrary pricing, veracity in advertising, gender issues in the workplace (beyond the legal issues of sexual harassment and glass ceilings), economic conflicts of interest, plus outsourcing and downsizing to the extent that the lives of both employees and patients are "upfouled."

Medical Bioethics

The brave new world of medical bioethics includes but is not limited to concern with genetic engineering and gene therapy, reproductive biology issues including stem cell research and human cloning, sale of human body parts for transplantation, and questions of intellectual ownership. Should new gene therapy modalities be patented in the same way drug companies can patent new pharmaceutical discoveries?

In addition, ethicists and nanotechnology experts are now debating the question of whether or not nanotechnology raises new ethical concerns.

In the next chapter, we'll take a look at how a health care ethicist might apply the tools in the ethicist's toolbox (ethical schools of thought, ethical principles, moral values, critical thinking, and persuasive argumentation) to health care's difficult situations (ethical dilemmas).

Reference

1. Robert T. Hall. *An Introduction to Healthcare Organizational Ethics*. Oxford, England, and New York, N.Y.: Oxford University Press, 2000, p. vii.

Chapter 8

How to Think and Argue Like a Health Care Ethicist

This chapter alone might prove to be worth the price you paid for this manual, because it is a roadmap. Even the best ethics committees can get lost sometimes and may need a roadmap to help them get back on track. Take this roadmap with you to meetings of the Ethics Committee. Would you read a roadmap and then leave it behind when you take the trip?

The features on this roadmap include:

- Four ethical principles
- Five moral values
- Three specific considerations

This construct, a balanced combination of ethical principles and moral values, is patterned after but does not exactly mirror the suggestions of Beauchamp and Childress.[1] Criticisms of the Beauchamp and Childress model are primarily about philosophical ethical theory, not about day-to-day practical usefulness of this approach.

In passing, note that it is tempting to use the term, *moral intelligence* to refer to this balanced approach, although the term is already in use in other contexts.

Four Ethical Principles

In health care ethics, four key ethical principles are autonomy, nonmaleficence, beneficence, and justice.[1]

Autonomy

Think self-determination. Autonomy is an important ethical aspect of issues such as informed consent, electively interrupting a pregnancy, living wills, and the four kinds of euthanasia.

Autonomy implies both liberty (freedom from interference) and agency (the ability to act on one's own behalf). It is a cornerstone of the rights-based health care ethic so popular today.

Indeed, focusing on autonomy has forced parts of the Hippocratic Oath into obsolescence. See the related article, "I Swear By Hippocrates, The Hippocratic Oath is Dead," on the CD that accompanies this book.

The part of the Hippocratic Oath in question states: "I shall…according to my ability and judgment…[do that which] I consider of benefit to my patients, and abstain from whatever is deleterious and mischievous.[2]

Today, rather than doing what the doctor thinks is best for the patient, doctors are encouraged to do what the patient thinks is best for himself or herself. Thus some consider the above language in the Hippocratic Oath paternalistic, which is a trigger word indicating to some an invasion of a patient's autonomy.

A debatable question is, "Is this not another place to apply 'all things in moderation?' In other words, to what extent should patients be in charge of decisions about their own care?" When Jo, my wife, was deciding last year between hemodialysis and hospice, at one point she burst out: "Why does everybody keep telling me, 'It's all up to you!?' I am so tired of being told, 'This is all up to you!'"

The practitioner most people want today is the one with good interpersonal skills who knows how to engage in a mutual decision-making process with patients. A trusted doctor or nurse who is a good communicator must provide accurate clinical information needed by a patient or surrogate decision-maker who is considering diagnostic and treatment options.

Nonmaleficence

Upon entering medical school, students are taught first thing, "Above all, be a safe physician. *Primum non nocere*." Above all, do no harm. This nonmaleficence must also guide other health care professionals and hospital management.

For example:

- When selecting an antibiotic, safety first. Then consider effectiveness, then cost. Unfortunately, a cheaper generic drug is not a viable option if it is not as safe and effective as its brand name counterpart. That is a major flaw, by the way, in the details of Part D Medicare Drug Plans, the ethical aspects of which have not been examined, to my knowledge

- When deciding whether or not to recommend an operation, be fully aware of any secondary medical problems that might increase the patient's surgical risk.
- Before closing down the newborn intensive care unit because it is a money-loser, consider the community's need for such a unit;
- When considering possible cost-cutting measures, don't even think about having physicians sign a gag order. Hiding needed information from the patient might not be maleficent in and of itself, but what if the hidden information prevents proper patient care and thus leads to a poor patient care result?

Beneficence

Think benevolence, think do good; think achieve positive results.

Benevolence is an important aspect of almost every health care scenario, ranging from individual patient care encounters to a government's choice of health care policy. Without benevolence, without care, without compassion, what would patient care be like?

Justice

Think fairness. Think consistency. Think, to some degree, in some situations, "If it's the rule for him or her, then it's the rule for me, too."

Two competing theories of justice are egalitarianism (John Rawls) and entitlement (Robert Nozicki).

Egalitarianism indicates equality by some measure. Ah, there's the rub; what is the measure? In providing health care services, and/or in a national health care policy, does equality mean universal—every citizen is entitled to every available service as a handout? Such an interpretation of egalitarianism is at the root of socialist forms of government.

Or does equality mean equal opportunity? For example, should attempts to re-form (fundamentally change) health care policies be broader based? To finally get rid of the ill-advised employer-provided health care model, employers might have to accommodate more readily the notion of a living wage. Then, more U.S. citizens, including many of today's uninsured, would share in the opportunity to participate in a uniform national health care policy that required partial payment by patients.

A view of economic justice that opposes egalitarianism is entitlement. In this construct, money and goods should not be equally owned by all citizens. Rather, a fair distribution would be made according to effort and accomplishment. Robert

Nozick, ironically a colleague of Rawls at Harvard, argues for justice as entitlement by considering the case of Wilt Chamberlain.

Chamberlain is one of the greatest university and professional basketball players of all time. It is only fair that Wilt Chamberlain make more money than his teammates, argues Nozick, because he is more skilled. And chances are, if the foundation salary base is reasonable, Wilt's teammates will not complain and demand equal pay. After all, is it not Wilt's drawing power that keeps the team in business and profitable and thus secures the salaries of all players?

As you think of applying these two views of justice to specific situations, you might conclude again that there are few if any absolutes in ethics. Perhaps egalitarian ethics fits one fact situation whereas entitlement is more applicable to another matter being simultaneously decided. Or, once again, perhaps the best choice is a synthesis, in this case a combination of equal opportunity and entitlement.

Five Moral Values[3]

The Difference between Ethical Principles and Moral Values

Ethical principles are tools used in an intellectual examination of a difficult situation, a process known as ethical reasoning. Ethical reasoning is a special application of critical thinking, Uncommon sense. Usually, ethical reasoning can lead to justification of more than one ethical choice in a difficult situation (ethical dilemma).

Moral values reflect a person's sense of what is right (angelic) and wrong (evil). Our moral values determine which of several ethical solutions we select. Often closely held moral values and personal beliefs are based less on logic and the law than they are based on experience and emotion.

Example

Closing a money-losing high-risk newborn unit is logically ethical if utilitarian principles are followed, because money can be diverted to the care of other patients. The principle of benevolence is also served, from the viewpoint of stakeholders other than newborns who are now able to receive previously non-funded services. On the other hand, closing the unit is unethical if one considers the supreme good to be the value of every human life. Newborn stakeholders and their families will be left out in the cold.

What to do, what to do? Using moral values, we can first eliminate unthinkable choices. It would be unethical and immoral, not to mention illegal, to close down the newborn ICU and then siphon the savings into our personal bank accounts.

And in the end, our moral values will determine whether we close the money-losing newborn ICU or leave it open. If we value the good of hospital operations in general, no pun intended, more than we value the life of newborns, we will close the unit. However, if we value the life of each newborn ahead of the general good of hospital operations *in this particular instance*, we will find some way to keep the unit open.

I say again, ethical reasoning without an underpinning of moral values is an empty exercise.

Five generally accepted moral values (some call them moral virtues) applicable to health care issues are:

Caring

Think empathy, compassion, a wish to create a benevolent result. Think: A feeling of discomfort and sadness at the misfortunes dealt to some as part of the human condition.

Caring and absolute altruism are not synonyms. Caring does not require the sacrifice of one's own well-being to alleviate the suffering of others. However, caring does require that the suffering of others be of some concern to us.

Caring and justice are closely related, but caring usually implies more personal involvement, more personal commitment, than justice.

Awareness

Think recognition. Ethics committee members must recognize and acknowledge facts clearly in evidence, facts that affect all stakeholders in a situation, and future possible unwanted adverse results of decisions and actions. None of these factors should be ignored.

Trustworthiness

The doctor-patient relationship is based on trust, and so is the hospital-community-relationship. Without trust, there can be neither stable long-range relationships nor sustainable market share.

Integrity

Integrity is a matter of consistent dependability, telling everyone the same thing, keeping promises, that sort of thing.

Duty/Obligation/Commitment

Kantian duty/obligation is often an applicable principle in health care, as is Aristotelian virtue. I would suggest accountability as a synonym, but that word is so connected with compliance behavior that I hesitate to use it in this ethical context.

Basically, when we talk about duty, we are talking about the will to do what is right, after thinking carefully about what is the right thing to do. Another term for this characteristic is responsibility.

Three Specific Considerations

Additional considerations include but are not necessarily limited to

- Privacy
- Information/informed consent
- Security

Privacy

In health care settings, at least four kinds of privacy are important:

Informational privacy—Think HIPAA, the Health Insurance Portability and Accountability Act. Most agree that it is inappropriate for people to go snooping around personal medical information without express permission. In passing, note that HIPAA regulations are a wonderful example of the difference between compliance behavior and true internally driven ethical character. Compulsive but pro forma compliance with sometimes inappropriately targeted regulations is not at all the same as a genuinely motivated effort to decide which patient information should be kept confidential.

If Jack has AIDS, how do we resolve the dilemma of whether or not to report that fact, in order to prevent spread of the disease? On the other hand, if someone who is not on Jack's list but is a family member walks up and wants to know if Jack has arrived in the clinic yet, should we tell her? Are those questions of equal importance? Is it appropriate to treat those two questions identically, as HIPAA compliance procedures often do?

Do such questions not whet the appetite of inquisitive members of your ethics committee?

Physical Privacy—One human need and human right is dignity. Pretend you are the patient. In ways you would appreciate yourself, help the patient preserve dignities in matters of dress, avoidance of extraneous noise, personal hygiene, and respect shown by doctors, nurses, therapists, aides, technicians, housekeepers, the admission and finance offices, etc.

What do you think of this idea? Should the ethics committee be involved in efforts at maintaining respect for patient's physical privacy? Or is this none of the ethics committee's business?

Decisional privacy—The concept of decisional privacy is an extension of autonomy. The ethics committee should attempt to help medical staff members learn and understand interpersonal communication skills necessary to make patients and family members feel involved in choices of diagnostic and therapeutic modalities.

Should the ethics committee accept this challenge? Or is this none of the ethics committee's business?

Decisional privacy becomes a social agenda item and thus a political football in issues such as purposeful interruption of a pregnancy and assisted self-determination.

Note the attempt to demonstrate encouraging reasonable, calm discussion by using words other than traditional red flag trigger words. Purposeful interruption of pregnancy (PIP) is abortion. Assisted self-determination has up to now been referred to as assisted suicide. Words such as "killing" and "suicide" are emotionally charged and do little to inform reasoned debate on these subjects.

Proprietary privacy—Think the right to ownership of money and property; think John Locke; thus again think human rights.

Proprietary privacy has taken on a whole new meaning in the emerging age of genetic engineering and gene therapy. If a patient's genes would be curative when introduced into the body of another human, who owns the therapeutic genes and the process by which the cure is affected? Should therapeutic human genes be patented by companies in the same way as new discoveries and applications in traditional pharmacology can be patented? See the related article, "Does Patenting Genes Change the Meaning of Life?" on the CD accompanying this book.

Information/Informed Consent

The failure to provide enough information plus failure to confirm understanding prior to obtaining a patient's signature on an informed consent form continues to cause legal headaches for hospitals. A genuine intent to actually satisfy the intended objectives of informed consent could go a long way toward relieving those legal pressures.

Is that an ethical argument for high priority attention to being sure informed consent is truly informed? Or is it a legal argument? The answer is obvious, isn't it? An ethical argument for effective informed consent would focus on patients' rights to safety, demonstrating the professional ethic, truthfulness, integrity, and caring (compassion, beneficence).

Is informed consent the business of the ethics committee? Is information about hospital procedures encountered by the patient the business of the ethics committee? Without that information, of course, patients suffer fear of the unknown.

Security

Concern for patient safety is not limited to avoiding medication errors and mistakes in the operating suite. Security includes the same kind of safety that makes us lock our doors at night and keep valuables hidden or in a safe.

Encourage employees to challenge strangers loitering in patient care areas. Encourage caregivers to safeguard hospitalized patients' valuables that cannot be sent home, such as false teeth and eyeglasses.

Are these matters potential agenda items for the ethics committee? Or are these matters none of the ethics committee's business?

Now that we have populated our health care ethicist's tool box and provided ourselves with a road map, it seems logical and natural next to examine the questions: Why have an Ethics Committee? What does a 21st Century Ethics Committee do? Who should be on the Ethics Committee?

References

1. Tom Beauchamp and James Childress. *Principles in Medical Bioethics, 5th Edition*. New York and Boston: Harvard University Press, 2001. Chapters 3-6, pp. 57-282.

2. The Hippocratic Oath, 500 B.C. See Richard E. Thompson, MD, "I swear by Apollo, the Hippocratic Oath Is Obsolete." *Physician Executive* 30(2):60-3, March-April, 2004.

3. Anita L. Allen. "Genetic privacy: Emerging concepts and Values," in Mark A.Rothstein, Editor, *Genetic Secrets: Protecting Privacy and Confidentiality in the Genetic Era*. New Haven, Conn.: Yale University Press, 1997, pp. 31-59.

Part IV

About the Hospital's 21st Century Ethics Committee

Chapter 9

The Ethics Committee: Why Have One, What Does It Do, and Who Is on the Committee?

Do we really need an Ethics Committee? Believe it or not, this question truly deserves an answer, because some have suggested that supporting an Ethics Committee is not necessary in today's modern hospitals. Are they correct? Is your Ethics Committee truly necessary?

Hospital leaders are not very good at dealing with the first question that should be asked about every existing committee: Is this committee truly necessary? We are, instead, accustomed to complying with regulations and standards that are most easily met by creating and supporting a committee. So it is more in our nature to create committees and support the committee than to ever consider that some committee we have created might now be unnecessary.

Let's take a look at some reasons to have a committee and see which ones apply to the Ethics Committee. By the way, here comes a bonus you didn't expect when you bought this book, which is written by an old former medical staff organizational consultant. If you like the following process, which can be applied to any existing committee, then why limit its use to evaluating the need for the Ethics Committee?

Committees that exist for the following reasons may indeed be extraneous:

- It's traditional. This is the Is/Ought fallacy in action. "We have had this committee for years; that's the way it is and so that's the way it ought to be."

- If the committee is disbanded, people staffing the committee will be put out of work. We might have to downsize management staff. There's an opening. Fewer layers of management might be a better idea in health care organizations than reducing FTE's in the Nursing Service. However, the key point is...Disbanding a committee never puts people out of work. People staffing regular monthly meetings of a committee are often among the first to be glad to see a committee go. They have plenty of other items on their job description to fill the day!

- We need to have enough committees so that everybody can be on one and thus "pull their share of the load," organizationally speaking. Now I have betrayed my bona fides. Think old traditional, now nearly obsolete, organized hospital medical staff, once my main area of consulting activity. Thank goodness, (Hugh Greeley and I and others will take a small bow), this bad reason for having a committee became obsolete before the beginning of the 21st Century.

- We need to kill time. In some matters, rapid decision making is not the goal. That is, decision makers are benefiting from some situation that, if changed, would benefit someone else instead. In hospitals, perhaps in any organization, there is no better way to act slowly than to refer the matter to a committee.

- The committee exists because leaders think that the committee is required, but no such requirement actually exists. To this day, needless committees exist in hospitals because those responsible for achieving JCAHO accreditation over-interpret, misinterpret, or simply do not read the exact language of JCAHO standards and interpretative information.

If your Ethics Committee exists for any of these reasons, you may not need it.

Good reasons to have a committee include but are not necessarily limited to:

- The authority of the committee is needed. In hospitals, this is seldom a good reason to keep a committee. We have too many bosses and too few workers in hospitals as it is. We don't need to further complicate the definition of relative responsibility and authority. This is no reason to keep the Ethics Committee.

- The agenda of a larger group is too busy to handle all the items with which the larger committee must deal. Think Board Committees. This is not relevant to the Ethics Committee. We don't need one for this reason.

- The work of the committee cannot be accomplished better in any other way. Committees that once existed to review data and/or primary source patient records, analyze findings, draw conclusions, and decide action steps all in the space of an hour or two are perfect examples of this principle. Why wouldn't month-long activities of responsible individuals be better than monthly meetings of an Ethics Committee?

- The expertise and input of multiple disciplines is needed. This is often quoted as a reason to keep the Ethics Committee. True, ethics is a complex area, and it is necessary to employ insights from many professions and viewpoints. However, is getting together in a monthly meeting the best way to do this? Often, the committee member needed for a specific agenda item can't make it to a meeting. Just as often, we discover that it was foolish to think that we could anticipate every committee need when we appointed committee members at the start of the year. We work ad hoc anyway, don't we, often inviting in people with needed expertise who are not regular committee members?

- Since the invention of telephones, pooling expertise has not been a good reason to hold a monthly committee meeting. Today this point is even stronger. You have never heard of e-mail?

- Committee members must discuss a case. Again, you have never heard of e-mail? You have never heard of blogs and various kinds of chat rooms? I am currently teaching an online Health Care Ethics course. The students and I are having some great discussions. We have never met each other face to face and probably never will. Indeed, all students could not make it to a meeting even if we called one. One student, for example, is in Iraq. I am currently ending a term on the editorial board of the *Springfield News and Leader*. We have some great discussions, *on line*. The need to discuss is no longer a good reason to keep a committee.

- With respect to needing to come to consensus (not vote, usually) on a recommendation...Hmmmmm...

  Come to think of it, the editorial board meets once a month to decide on group input on some issues. When we interviewed candidates before the last elections, we met and did that in a group. In the online course, the students and I don't meet, but the online faculty does. Not monthly, but we meet.

  There may be no better way to have needed deliberations of the Ethics group than to call ourselves a formal committee and schedule a meeting time that committee members might be able to save on their busy calendars. But is this need alone reason to keep the formal committee?

- Assigning a task performed by the committee to an individual would be unfair, because it puts too much strain on one person. Hmmmmm. We are going to recommend whether or not to discontinue life support. We may need to challenge the powers that be about a dishonest ad or a lack of justice in dealing with employees. All who want to stand up and do this alone, without support, raise your hands?

- The work of most committees is not this emotionally charged. Group support for individuals involved in ethical dilemmas is another good reason to have a standing mechanism such as the Ethics Committee available in the organization.

- The committee is required. At least with respect to the Joint Commission on Accreditation of Health Care Organizations (JCAHO), an Ethics Committee is no longer required, if indeed it ever was. JCAHO's new patient-centered survey and accreditation exercise include attention to ethics and patients' rights, but the role of a committee is optional, up to each surveyed institution. Few if any Ethics Committees exist simply because of the mistaken notion that this committee is required.

At the bottom line, it doesn't take a long list of reasons to justify the existence of a committee. The frequent need to achieve consensus, the need for multidisciplinary activity in those deliberation sessions, the need for emotional support, the need for a buffer to inform decision makers in an individual clinical case, the need to have regular ECC (Ethics Continuing Education) sessions, and the need for a united front when confronting hospital management about matters such as the unintended negative impact of an ill-advised ad or the imposition of gag orders all suggest that the Ethics Committee is indeed a useful hospital organizational mechanism.

After all that, here is actually the quickest and simplest way to find out if you truly need the Ethics Committee. At the next Ethics Committee meeting, make this announcement: "I have good news. The Ethics Committee is hereby disbanded. I know you are pleased, because you, like I, occasionally complain about how many committee meetings we have to attend every month. Now you and I have one less! It has been wonderful working with you. Thank you so much for your support. The meeting is now adjourned."

That announcement should rock the boat. If you don't see any waves, then you don't truly need the Ethics Committee.

That's What I Think, Now Here's How I Feel

I have shared my thinking, now I will share my feelings. I would not seriously consider a recommendation to do without an Ethics Committee unless the recommendation is the pooled opinion of front-line practitioners from several disciplines. Consider this personal experience:

Twins are born prematurely. Many premature babies go on to become robust, healthy, intelligent, productive adults. However, in the case of one of these twins, signs of brain damage are already evident. This will not be a productive, happy life, the way most of us define those terms. And here comes an additional tragic detail. The mother of the twins is thirteen years old and the biological father is her adopted 13-year-old brother. Is that last factor relevant to deciding whether or not to turn off the respirator?

I actually faced and resolved that dilemma as a pioneer neonatologist in the early 1970s, before ethics committees were commonplace. I made the decision to turn off the respirator alone, unaided by guidelines, relevant precedents, or running my decision by a knowledgeable and caring but detached group, who could afford to be totally objective in their recommendation. Today, as one ACPE member recently commented on the online ACPE Ethics Forum, such a decision without benefit of a recommendation by the ethics committee would actually be suspect.

No wonder I'm a big fan of ethics committees.

What Does an Ethics Committee Do?

Ethics committee members, working with and through their designees and resource persons:

- Educate
- Consult
- Review
- Recommend

Have you learned anything new from this primer and practical guidebook so far? Whether the answer to that question is yes or no, is there a need for education about what's happened to ethics in general and to health care ethics in particular throughout your organization? Do materials need to be prepared or does oral patient orientation information need to include advising patients and family members that there is a Hospital Ethics Committee?

Increasing awareness of ethics is a major task of the ethics committee. And the task is not easy. Some people think they know all they ever want to know about ethics and then some took a university ethics class and it was boh-ring, boh-ring, boh-ring. Those people might be pleasantly surprised to learn that what they know about ethics is actually now the history of ethics. Make them aware that 21st Century practical ethics applied can be a valuable and dynamic part of the decision-making process for managers and executives, and a dynamic part of caring for patients if one is a health care professional.

What do physicians know about ethics? Some know a lot; some know very little either because they are not interested or because they have never had an opportunity to learn.

Physician education is a very special application of adult continuing education because working with physicians is like herding cats. One management consultant has even likened working with physicians to driving a dynamite truck. Many physicians hate…carefully chosen word…this feeling is very strong…hate the notion that someone is attempting to intervene "between me and *my* patient."

These days, are physicians the only health care professionals who speak, justifiably, of *my* patient? The answer is obvious, isn't it?

If a team of health care professionals and/or a patient and family members would like an ethics consult, then it behooves the physician to allow it. However, because the order sheet is in some settings still the sole property of duly licensed MDs and DOs, little can be done with patients without an order from, or at least without the specific approval of, a patient's attending physician.

Educating physicians is one of the Ethics Committee's most important and most difficult tasks. We physicians are hard to educate, because we are famous for thinking that we know everything. Do you know how many doctors it takes to change a light bulb? Only one. The doctor stands on a chair and holds the light bulb while the whole world revolves around him or her.

However, take heart. Many physicians are excellent students, if they become interested in some area of study. The key to educating physicians is motivating them to learn. Well, isn't that the key for everyone?

Avoid trying to find one global approach to motivating "the medical staff." The only way to educate a group of doctors is to take time to find out what makes each doctor tick.

In addition, keep your expectations reasonable. In spite of your best efforts, only a few physicians will participate in your educational activities. And that's all you need! These few will spread the word to other physicians. For years, working in areas such as credentialing and medical staff bylaws, I enjoyed educating a few key physicians then watching them educate their peers. I apologize to non-physicians readers and users of this book for the fact that, to this day, some physicians will listen only to other physicians.

Educating the hospital's practicing physicians is extremely important to ethics committee success. Especially in the area of providing ethics consultation in specific clinical cases, objections of the attending physician, a consulting physician, or an operating surgeon is sometimes a major roadblock to overcome.

Don't forget to educate yourselves! Self-education and CEE (Continuing Ethics Education) should be high on the committee's priority list.

Consider offering committee members a 30-minute educational session in conjunction with the committee's business meetings. In addition, consider offering an annual or semi-annual educational retreat for ethics committee members. This could be set up in such a way that it is a perk of committee membership, but it need not be.

Actually, when on the medical staff leadership/board/executive seminar and retreat circuit, I discovered that many doctors actually preferred a concentrated Saturday morning seminar, 9 am to 1 pm with free lunch after and no afternoon session. Also, many physicians preferred a location in or close to the hospital rather than a contrived combination of business and pleasure a la the proverbial and legendary weekend retreat mode. If physicians want to go away for the weekend, they will go away for the weekend. And when they do, many prefer going to a place of their own choosing, being with their own choice of companions, and being free of the need to rush through a morning seminar to make a scheduled tee time.

Provide educational opportunities to the hospital's nursing leaders and department directors. Consider some form of ethics education for grass roots personnel.

What about the senior executive staff? The good news is that this group may engage the subject matter and interact with you in a useful and productive way. The bad news is: When the doors to the executive suite and board room close, senior organizational leaders may see little connection between what they have learned about ethics and many difficult items on management's agenda.

Ethics Consultation Regarding a Current Clinical Case

A family wants the doctor to turn off grandpa's respirator so that he will no longer suffer. Or is that the real reason? And do all family members agree? Chances are, the family is split down the middle. A pro-life cousin is accusing a compassionate son of defying the will of God. A greedy cousin favors pulling life support, eager to get at the fortune the old man is sitting on.

In such scenarios, the doctor is in the middle, feeling the squeeze. Where can he or she go to get some help, support, expertise including awareness of relevant hospital policies, and relief from the burden of being the sole decision-maker in this case? Enter the ethics committee.

A special word to you and previous ethics committee members who have done such good work for so many years now: The suggestion that the modern-day hospital ethics committee expand its activities in no way implies a lesser need for ethics consultation in individual clinical cases.

Other Kinds of Consultations

Public Image Consultation

Encourage senior management and the board to ask your view of plans, proffered services, the annual budget, credentialing decisions, advertisements. The idea is to tell decision-making leaders how their decisions, actions, etc. look to stakeholders such as patients and potential patients, advocates of strictly regulating the health care industry, community businesses, and the hospital's employees. Why create negative press and a less than desirable reputation when a negative image, injurious to marketing efforts, can be avoided?

In the utilitarian tradition, senior management might decide to implement its decision anyway, because the good organizational result achieved will outweigh anticipated negative attendant results.

Is it not better if senior management expects only net good, as opposed to being disappointed because the absolute good expected, unjustifiably, was not achieved?

Review of Policies and Procedures

Hospital department directors should be made aware that the ethics committee will, on request, analyze existing and proposed policies and procedures and provide a report on perceived ethical issues therein.

I cannot over-emphasize the following: If self-education of committee members includes training in the ability to provide reports of their analysis of ethical aspects of a policy in a helpful and non-judgmental way, you might develop a good reputation and have many chances to impact positively on the wording and implementation of various policies and procedures. This would be simultaneously beneficial for the organization, its leaders, patient care professionals, and patients and their family members.

On the other hand, if ethics committee members see the phrase "review a policy" and lapse into the old, familiar negative, legalistic meaning of those words…if you act like a regulator or a surveyor or an attorney, don't worry about being overworked in your role as an ethics committee member.

Public Policy Recommendations

Do any features of state or federal law throw up roadblocks when you try to help the hospital's professional staff with difficult matters, such as end-of-life issues? Should any laws and regulations relevant to your work as an ethics committee member be changed? If so, do you choose to make timely and relevant political activity part of your ethics committee's agenda or not? Is such political effort a good contribution because of the expertise you develop from dealing with real issues constantly? Or does your close involvement with controversial health care matters, some of them popular political footballs, make your committee's voice a prejudiced one, in one direction or the other?

The choice of whether or not to add political activity to your ethics committee's list of activities is entirely up to you, or to the intra-organizational authority to which or to whom you are accountable.

Who Should Be on the Ethics Committee?

The composition of the ethics committee should be described/defined in a relevant governance document or policy manual. However, it is a mistake to take the same compulsive and legalistic approach to committee "composition" as is necessary when complying with specifically stated requirements.

Decide:

1. What disciplines should be represented on the ethics committee?
2. What personal characteristics should be looked for in a potential ethics committee member?

A Multidisciplinary Committee

By definition, the ethics committee must include members of several different disciplines. That is, one major goal of ethics and ethical reasoning is to consider the interests and concerns of all stakeholders in a difficult situation, so we need to take pains to be sure all stakeholders' interests are recognized.

For example, I can tell you from experience as a medical staff consultant, get a group of us doctors together and we are very likely to ignore, however inadvertently, the concerns of co-workers like nurses, technicians, and therapists.

In the same way, a committee composed completely of health care insiders might, however inadvertently, misrepresent the actual needs and concerns of patients and their family members.

On the other hand, set up an ethics committee composed completely of "public representatives," and I'll show you a group that may end up making faulty decisions because of unfamiliarity with some of the realities of daily clinical decision making and patient care.

In deciding what disciplines to include on the ethics committee, consider needed expertise. Today's medical bioethical issues are complex, requiring knowledge and accurate application of ethical principles and moral values, but also of economic and political realities, and of scientific fact. Indeed, scientific fact must come first!

To some extent the committee can rely upon invited experts to provide situation-specific expertise. However, ongoing smooth functioning of the committee is probably best ensured by including a variety of disciplines on the list of committee members.

Most hospital ethics committees would include physicians, nurses, hospital department heads, grass roots employees, clergy, social services specialists, and public representatives. Committee composition might also include a board member. The participation of attorneys in the ethics committee's deliberations might be as full members, or as invited consultants to offer information about legal aspects of situations, where that is necessary. Be sure the attorney does not mislead you by inadvertently conflating ethical issues and legal issues.

When choosing members for the Ethics Committee, survey the hospital and the community to discover a local treasure. This treasure would be an individual well-versed in modern-day health care ethics, whether that individual is an ethicist or just well-read. Invite that person's participation either as a full-time member of the committee or as an occasional consultant and educator.

Personal Characteristics of a Good Ethics Committee Member

A good (competent, contributing) member of an ethics committee will be:

- Chomping at the bit to help make ethical behavior a high priority throughout the organization.

- Busy, but not so busy that he or she is not available for committee meetings and occasional special assignments.

- Cooperative, a brain-storming problem-solver in meetings as opposed to a position-taking, zealous advocate who controls a meeting by provoking, intimidating, and distracting.

- Articulate, in both writings and oral communication.
- Well-respected. If those working in the hospital, top to bottom and side to side, cannot respect members of the ethics committee, with which they most likely have daily dealings, why should they respect the efforts of the committee?

Chapter 10

Some Organizational Details

What is the ethics committee's organizational location? That is, by what authority is the ethics committee established, and to what individual or group does the committee report?

Does the committee and/or its chair have line authority in any areas, or does the committee depend on the authority of another individual or group to carry out its recommendations?

Are there any ex officio members of the Ethics Committee, with or without vote? Is the President of the Medical Staff a member? Is the VPMA (Vice President for Medical Affairs)? Is the CEO or an immediate designee a member of the committee?

What is the assigned role of legal counsel? Or is the ethics committee none of the hospital attorney's business?

If there is a corporate office ethics committee, and/or an individual in the corporate office whose responsibilities include organizational ethics and related matters, what is the working relationship of the hospital's ethics committee to that corporate committee or responsible individual?

How does the work of the committee get done, and who does it?

What organizational mechanism is used to ensure easy access to the committee when a team of health care professionals needs to request an ethics consultation on a current clinical case?

What are the information reporting lines of the ethics committee? Who makes regular reports to the ethics committee, and to whom does the ethics committee provide routine reports?

What is the relationship of the Ethics Committee to the hospital's IRB (Institutional Review Board)? The IRB is charged with assuring safety of human research subjects, insofar as is humanly possible.

In what governance documents and/or policy and procedure manuals are the answers to these and other organizational questions located?

This primer and practical guide does not presume to provide detailed answers to the above questions. One reason is that there is little if any need, because those details are well in place in most hospitals. If there is one thing we are good at it is building organizational structure!

In addition, long ago I became leery of providing too many specific forms and methods descriptions, because I found that some people using a manual like this got the notion that they should discard perfectly fine methods and forms they had devised themselves to use what an "expert" recommends. Never forget, an ex is a has-been and a spurt is a drip under pressure. Your own ideas are fine as long as they work for you.

However, before we go on…

Please use the list of questions above as a checklist. Be sure you can find an answer to each question in your existing organizational system. If you cannot, put your hands in the air in a "Time Out" sign, and update structural details.

By the way, the update/revision need not take months of meetings. Prepare recommendations, discuss them with two or three committee leaders, fine tune them, take them to the next meeting for a first reading and to the meeting after that for approval. This suggestion assumes the purpose of effective and efficient organization, not an effort to give the Ethics Committee direct authority over anything or anybody.

I don't want to talk any more about structure. Too many times we make structural considerations an end point when they are not. At the bottom line, I wish to focus your attention on function. I wish to guide your thinking, without offering you the opportunity to skip over all of this primer and practical guidebook except a section containing forms and policies to be photocopied and adopted. Don't think attention to structure is a day's work. Ethics requires a deeper approach than that.

This chapter will content itself with offering suggestions about three details of Ethics Committee structure/policy and methods/procedure. Those three details are:

- Organizational location of the Ethics Committee
- A possible need for three subcommittees
- The need for an Ethics Committee Liaison

Organizational Location of the Ethics Committee

The ethics committee should be a committee of the board. That way, the authority of the committee and top-level organizational support for the committee are clearly visible in the organization, top to bottom and side to side.

Boards have fiduciary responsibility (ultimate responsibility) for the dependability and safety of organizational products and services, as well as for money. Therefore, this suggestion does not seem far-fetched.

A board representative should be an ex officio member of the Ethics Committee, with or without vote.

The description of committee composition might call for the board member to serve for six months, then give way to another board member who serves on the ethics committee for six months, and so on. That is one good way to fairly quickly increase the number of board members who have a good idea, even an intimate inside idea, of what's going on in the way of attention to ethics in the hospital.

The board representative would report ethics committee activities to the board on a regular basis. Or, the board representative would help the Ethics Committee chair prepare and present reports to the board.

In addition, an executive such as the Vice President for Medical Affairs or his or her designee might be an ex officio member of the Ethics Committee.

The idea of the Ethics Committee being a committee of the board might not be palatable. The idea of board and executive members of the committee might seem strange to you. If so, please come up with some alternative way to ensure, insofar as possible, that the ethics committee is not a distant stepchild housed in the hospital basement next to the boiler room.

The major mistakes to avoid in terms of establishing organizational details are:

- Don't establish the ethics committee in medical staff bylaws. Mention it in medical staff bylaws but don't establish it there. This is not a medical staff committee. Avoid in every way possible giving physician leaders the idea that ownership of this committee is theirs. Their participation is indispensable, but this is not just another "medical staff committee."

- Don't look around the organization, decide ethics is a lot like regulatory compliance, and add ethics to the job description of the VP in charge of complying with regulations. Ethics and compliance require a different knowledge base, different attitudes, different people skills, and a different relationship with the hospital's executive and management staff, medical staff, nursing staff, patients and family members, and the community.

- Don't look around the organization and decide that, because ethics and the law are inextricably intertwined (they are!), surely the best decision is to add staffing the Ethics Committee to the duties of the Risk Manager or in-house legal counsel. Ethics and the Law are first cousins, but they are not identical twins. There is no better way to ensure unwanted conflation of ethical aspects and legal aspects of a difficult situation than to have responsibility for ethics and legal matters housed in the same individual, the same office, and/or the same organizational structure.

Consider Establishing Three Subcommittees

One good reason to have subcommittees is, the agenda of the full committee is too crowded for the full committee to deal effectively with all matters relevant to the committee's responsibilities.

It may be time to appoint three subcommittees of the Ethics Committee along the lines suggested by the Three Faces of Health Care Ethics. That is:

- The Traditional Medical Ethics Subcommittee
- The Organizational Ethics Subcommittee
- The Medical Bioethics Subcommittee

The Ethics Committee Liaison

The Ethics Committee Liaison is a person. He or she is the answer to the question, "How can I gain access to the Ethics Committee if I need help?"

Ideally, the liaison (add "s" if you want to appoint two or more who can then arrange an on-call schedule among themselves) should be a person with a unique combination of attributes. First and foremost, the person must be respected and must be a good communicator. Next, the liaison ideally will have a special interest in and some expertise in the field of health care ethics. Finally, the liaison will understand that his or her primary purpose is to make it easy for all throughout the organization to call on the ethics committee when help is needed. Almost always, that will require timely availability. So, the liaison must be willing to be readily accessible. I am imagining that the liaison is a full member of the Ethics

Committee. Otherwise, the connection to the committee would seem loose and incomplete.

The liaison is not necessarily a physician, nurse or clergyperson, but individuals in these disciplines might be best suited to accept this responsibility. Equally likely in some settings is that an experienced Ethics Committee member who may not be a health care professional or religious professional would make an excellent liaison. Indeed, you might be thinking at this point that you already have a committee member who has accepted this responsibility and that this person fits this description.

If you recognize in the above a description of an existing informal mechanism, formalize it. Write up what you are doing and how you do it. Make each step, from calling the liaison to getting needed help, perfectly clear. Is completion of a written request necessary? What time frame is applicable? Surely the committee would not wait until the next monthly meeting to provide help in a current clinical ethical dilemma. Is the liaison permanently appointed, or does the duty rotate among qualified and willing committee members?

The details of this arrangement are entirely up to you. At the bottom line, establish some clear and publicized mechanism whereby people throughout the organization can call for help and get a timely response.

Chapter 11

Meeting Procedures and Standardized Agenda

On one hand, the Ethics Committee is a very special committee. Its members deal with non-routine situations of many kinds. Its deliberations and decisions can greatly affect the lives, work, and well-being of people thrown together by circumstance as patient, concerned family member, doctor, and nurse.

This committee's efforts to help keep organizational systems and goals ethical can be a key to gaining much needed public and political support, and even market share. At the bottom line, the truth is that visible displays of genuine interest in and concern about patients, family members, and the community sell very well.

On the other hand, there is nothing lofty and fine about the Ethics Committee at all. That is, the Ethics Committee and its members have the same operational problems as every other committee in the hospital. Busy members conscientiously arrive on time for the meeting, only to twiddle their thumbs while the committee chair waits "just a little longer" to start, to "see who else comes." Planners conflate the purposes of a business meeting and a dinner gathering, resulting in committee members' spending more time than necessary at the meeting, at the expense of dinner at home with their families.

Discussions that are hard to follow could be made more understandable with the use of a few simple visuals, such as handouts and projected PowerPoint® slides. Debates that should move in a straight line toward a moment of decision making become circular, and key speakers in the debate become less problem solvers and more position takers the longer the debate is allowed to continue.

I hasten to add, because the area of concern is ethics, efficient meeting is a relative term. Don't rush. The hardest part of being ethical may be taking time to think, because everything in our society informs us that speed is good.

As with any committee, a good meeting begins with good committee leadership skills and with how well committee members have been oriented to group process skills and techniques.

Here are some suggestions. Perhaps this chapter will prove an unexpected bonus, because there is no reason you cannot apply these ideas to every committee in the hospital.

- Meetings should begin five minutes after the announced meeting time. If a meal is involved, the meeting announcement should so indicate: Lunch at noon; Meeting begins at 12:20.
- Start the meeting by the clock, not by how many people are in the room at the announced starting time. If you start beginning on time, more committee members will start coming on time.
- No meeting should last longer than one hour and fifteen minutes. A one-hour meeting well attended is ordinarily more productive than long dragged out meetings that are poorly attended.
  - —If you can't finish the agenda in 75 minutes, work on better meeting preparation. For example, for action items on the agenda, prepare a list of three feasible possibilities for the group to discuss, rather than going cold into the meeting and asking, "Well, what do you want to do about this?"
  - —When possible, delegate tasks to individual members, who are charged with accomplishing the tasks between meetings. Then, use meeting time for a brief report of results. Indeed, most committee agendas include too little time for follow up of previous recommendations and assignments.
- Work on chairperson skills. Informally use some good ideas from Robert's Rules of Order:
  - —Ask members to make their points in three or four minutes or less. Don't be a compulsive clocker; just set the tone.
  - —Advise members that no one gets to speak twice on an issue (except for relevant follow-up questions and comments) until every member who wants to has spoken once. Make that a guideline, not a strict rule. Don't let "parliamentary procedure" become the issue. Just set the tone.
  - —Advise members to address comments and questions to the chair, not to each other. A good chairperson keeps control of the meeting and does not let side conversations distract and/or disturb the group.
  - —Advise members, "No yelling." Members are to present arguments, not quarrel. Members should be asked to keep a civil tongue at all times.
  - —Anyone chairing a meeting should keep two obligations in mind. One is to allow time for each member to speak his or her piece. However, the chair should also protect the time of members willing to attend meetings.

—Use visuals, because visuals help keep meeting participants on the same page, literally. Visuals aid understanding and thus improve the chances of good committee decisions efficiently arrived at.

—Hand out printed copies of the agenda.

—If a case is to be discussed, hand out a case summary, along with two or three discussion starter observations and questions.

—Hand out exact language of policies and recommendations the committee is asked to endorse or formally approve. By the way, yes, ideally you do send meeting materials to every committee member before the meeting and ideally every member will come into the meeting already knowing what's going on, and will bring the previously distributed materials with them.

—Send the materials, but also take copies to the meeting and be prepared to redistribute them. Plus, the chair should introduce each agenda item with a brief summary of what's in the materials. Where are the hot spots in the case or in data? What is the exact language of, and what is between the lines of, policies or propositions that the committee is asked to endorse?

—When putting a matter before the committee, indicate whether this is an action item or an information item. If the matter is an action item, indicate what action is expected: Recommend, approve, endorse, what? If the matter is an information item, indicate why this is something the committee needs to know, and what committee members are expected to do with the knowledge.

Stay on the Subject, Which Is Ethics

In the Ethics Committee's discussions/debates, occasionally ask yourself and each other, "Are we still on track?" In any discussion, sticking to the subject is difficult. When talking about ethics, keeping the discussion on track is even harder than usual. Avoid four common mistakes people make when they try to talk about ethics:

- Don't start talking ethics and end up talking religion. "Is this what God wants us to do?" is not a question about ethics, it is a question about religion. "We should recommend this because it is in line with the Ten Commandments and the Beatitudes," is not ethical reasoning. It is a religious argument. And remember, the patient under discussion might be Hindu, Islamic, or atheist.
- Do not misunderstand! I did not say religious considerations have no place in Ethics Committee discussions. *Au contraire!* Religion is an integral part of many difficult situations (ethical dilemmas). When that is true, arguably ethics committee recommendations should reflect the stakeholders' religious beliefs, not a

committee member's religious beliefs. And a committee member's strongly held religious beliefs should not be allowed to impair the committee member's ability to participate in ethical reasoning.

A reminder: Again I say, in situations where religious directives govern the activities of the Ethics Committee, ignore the above and heed the religious directives, however they may conflict with the patients' beliefs.

Now that I've written that, it looks strange to me. I include it because I have been on the board of a couple of Catholic health care systems and I know the importance to clergy of "establishing and maintaining the Catholic presence."

Is it the Ethics Committee's business to help ensure full disclosure? Are patients fully aware that Catholicism strictly governs some clinical decisions in areas not related to childbirth?

- Do not start talking ethics and end up talking economics. "I think it is ethical to legalize euthanasia; because the money we spend caring for the irreversibly ill and the elderly is straining our budget."
- Do not start talking ethics and end up talking politics. "We could endorse that board action, I guess, but if we do, would the City Council still approve our acquisition of the land on which to build the new, larger ambulatory care center?" Remember, your role is to consult and advise about ethical aspects of patient care encounters and organizational policies and plans.
- Do not start out talking ethics and end up talking about the law. This is very difficult, especially because case scenarios for discussion in learning situations are often ethical issues that have blown up into conflicts that had to be resolved by the courts. "I asked Fred, our hospital attorney, to come to this meeting and tell us if the Schiavo case is relevant precedent. I figure there is no need to re-invent the wheel."

  Do not misunderstand! Many, many ethical dilemmas have legal aspects in these days of rights ethics, interpreted as defense of our own rights rather than as respect for the rights of others. However, your difficult assignment is to avoid rehashing the discussion of legal issues, which is undoubtedly the focus of other meetings on the difficult situation. Your task is to add to the discussion the element of ethical reasoning.

At the bottom line, the point is not: Don't talk about these things. The point is: *Do not inadvertently segue from one consideration to another.*

What is the best way to avoid those errors?

When you want to add a comment about religious aspects of a situation to a committee discussion, start by saying, "This is a religious argument, I know, and I think in this particular case any discussion of what to do would be incomplete without acknowledging this point." Or, "In addition to the ethical objections we have raised to the hospital's misleading advertisement, isn't there the matter of whether or not we might be sued for deception in advertising or something? Shouldn't we ask legal counsel about this?"

Standardized Agenda

Standardized agendas are templates to use when planning the detailed agenda of a meeting. A standardized agenda with which you are probably familiar is found in Robert's Rules of Order:

Call to Order
Approve Minutes of Last Meeting
Old Business
New Business
Adjourn

A sample standardized agenda tailored to the activities of the ethics committee is show on page 74.

Immediately After the Meeting, Still in the Meeting Room

Some committee members stay to start talking with the committee's chairperson and staff about freshly assigned tasks, planning first steps and setting guideline dates.

In a football game, frequent committee meetings (huddles) are important but they are not the ball game. Nothing happens—no gains are made and the goal is not reached—until the players leave the huddle and go do their respective jobs.

It is the same in real life.

Standardized Agenda
Hospital Ethics Committee

1. *Pre-Meeting Activity: Last Minute Preparation*
   Before the meeting starts, the committee chair and those staffing the committee have a quick whisper session with each other to be sure neither plans any surprises for the other during the meeting. Plus, the chair and staff remind each member or guest presenting a report or proposal of the time allotted for the presentation and for discussion of this agenda item.

2. *Call the Meeting to Order*

3. *Introduce Invited Guests, If Any*
   An active Ethics Committee will frequently invite guests to attend one or more meetings of the committee. One invited guest might be an expert resource needed for discussion of a specific agenda item. Another invited guest might be a physician, nurse, executive, or department head who has asked for help and been given permission to present an issue to the committee and get some help.

4. *Read, Amend if Necessary, and Approve Minutes of the Last Meeting*
   Where have we been and where are we now?

5. *Reports*
   a. By committee members or other committee designees previously assigned specific tasks. Was the task accomplished? How? What was the result? Is the committee satisfied?
   b. By committee members who are liaison members, ex officio with or without vote, of other hospital committees and groups such as the IRB (Institutional Review Board), governing body planning and/or budget committee, credentials committee and/or other medical staff committees, nursing inservice education committee, etc.
   c. By senior executives, such as CEO, CFO, Vice President for Medical Affairs, Vice President of Nursing Services, etc., regarding matters that the ethics committee needs to know about because someone might request the committee's advice/input.
   d. Other reports, ad hoc, as relevant and needed.

6. *Old Business*
   Deliberations about unfinished agenda items from previous meetings.

7. *New Business*
   Presentations by guests seeking assistance with ethical aspects of a current issue or problem.
   Presentation of other matters not previously considered by the committee.

8. *Announcement of the date and place of the next meeting.*
   Will the next planned meeting be at the regularly appointed time and place?

9. *Adjourn*

Part V

Case Studies for Discussion: Traditional Medical Ethics

The chapters in Part V are designed to encourage individual study followed by group discussion. Use them as a resource for self-education activities of the ethics committee. Such activities should include all of the following:

- Informal discussions between meetings involving two or more ethics committee members, and perhaps others as well.
- Formally planned educational sessions (30-60 minutes) appended to the committee's regular monthly meetings.
- Three or four times a year, a Saturday morning seminar, which need be neither far from home nor expensive.

The Best Way to Learn Practical Ethics Applied

The best way to learn theoretical ethics is to read pages and pages of pontifical prose. However, the best way to learn practical ethics applied is to discuss cases chosen because they offer opportunities to learn about a frequently recurring dilemma and its ethical aspects.

The cases for discussion in this book are fictitious or happened elsewhere. That's the only way to go, because if you try to discuss actual cases ("Let's kill two birds with one stone; learn and get somewhere on this case"), you are likely to get nowhere twice as fast. That's because truly detached thinking, until you get the hang of it, requires that you have no stake in the case for discussion, and that you don't muddy the waters with personal beliefs.

Paste the following reminder on the forehead of every single committee member and committee staffer: When the objective is to learn and practice detached logical thinking (ethical reasoning), do not discuss cases that you are actually involved in, and for a moment lay your personal beliefs aside. However, when dealing with an actual case, be morally intelligent; check your detached logical conclusion against your (committee's) set of moral values.

I cannot over-emphasize the importance of separating these two steps, and of being honest with ourselves every step of the way. If we get the hang of this process and have enough moral turpitude (strength of character), even though by definition nothing we can decide or do will be 100% right, the solution we propose should be as right (correct, logical, responsive to observable facts) plus as right (angelic) as it is possible to imagine given the reality of existing circumstances.

By the way, you might be wondering: Are both steps really necessary? Here is one example of what can happen when one does not stop and think before deciding and acting according to heartfelt emotion and long-held personal beliefs (moral values):

In Missouri, in 2006, opponents of embryonic stem cell research mounted an effective scare campaign, raising the specter of human clones created from embryos grown *in vitro* to be a source of stem cells. Let's say that, emotionally, you feel, you believe, that a human clone is Frankenstein's monster and, furthermore, that only God should create human life. You go to the polls and vote against embryonic stem cell research.

Stop! Think first! At this writing, no one has yet successfully created a human clone. That doesn't mean it's not going to happen; it most likely *will* happen someday. But not using the same technology that is used to grow stem cells, because those cells will not grow any further even if you try.

In somatic cell nuclear transfer (SCNT), used in stem cell research, starter cells such as a skin cell or a blood cell are diploid…contain paired DNA chains. They are already partly differentiated…and by miracles of modern-day magic in the laboratory, they are made to reproduce themselves.

Human reproduction is a different process, because the starting point is not a somatic cell, it is a gamete, a reproductive cell, an egg or a sperm. Gametes are haploid…they contain only a single DNA chain. The important first step, the combining of two of those cells to form a zygote, provides critical DNA information to the reproducing cells that results in full development into a fetus that can then become an adult human.

In addition, human clones aren't just beamed up from a Petri dish, fully grown and clothed, the spitting image of the person from whom donor cells came. The creation of a human clone is similar to *in vitro* fertilization in that the embryo (don't picture a fetus with human characteristics; an embryo is a cell cluster) must be implanted into a surrogate mother and eventually come out a newborn. That will be true until people working on an artificial uterus have better success.

So without the critical thinking/ethical reasoning step, you would be voting on the basis of misinformation and scary futuristic science fiction. That's the right (angelic and correct) thing to do if your moral values tell you not to listen to the above explanation because it is the "voice of the Devil." That is the wrong (incorrect) thing to do, because stamping out embryonic stem cell research is not the way to prevent human cloning from becoming a reality.

By the way, if you attack that known fact on the basis of inadequate evidence, voila, there is a big argument in favor of stem cell research. All this furor about stem cells, when what we don't know about stem cells would fill a library.

Stop! Think!

Who Should Lead the Self-Educating Case Discussions

For full educational benefit, the case discussions must be facilitated by a knowledgeable and experienced resource person. To find such a person, first dip your buckets where you are. The person might be on the ethics committee, or a member might know an expert health care ethicist. A common mistake to avoid is to ask just any doctor, lawyer, or clergyman to take the point in ethics discussions. Granted, ethics is related to these fields and, if it's a matter of any port in a storm, then okay. However, professional category is far less important than knowledge of and experience with ethical aspects of 21st Century health care issues. Any physician, attorney, or clergyperson worth his or her salt will readily admit that not every member of their profession is interested in health care ethics.

Still looking for an expert ethicist to facilitate your educational discussions? Announce your need to the community, perhaps in a local newspaper feature about the committee and its activities. (That should be good public relations for the hospital). The person you need, perhaps a professor at the local university, might come forward to help, especially if you are willing to spring for a small stipend.

In addition to these efforts, ask each committee member to become expert in some area. Ask one member to read and present resource materials on living wills. Ask another to learn and explain the ins and outs of issues related to safety of human research subjects. Ask a committee member to lay the HIPAA regulations (legal aspects of protecting personal medical information) aside and discuss the ethical aspects of this issue.

How could a committee member fulfill such an assignment? Never underestimate the power of the Internet. Search the Internet for relevant topics. Google Scholar is a useful tool.

A caveat: "Use the Internet" is a potentially dangerous suggestion. Stop! Think! Carefully judge reliability of, root resources cited in, and objectivity of Internet sites! Watch out for sell jobs on controversial ethical issues, presented as objective fact.

Another idea is to get relevant resource materials from the Hastings Center (www.thehastingscenter.org), one of the nation's leading think tanks on health care ethics issues. The people at the Center are very approachable and willing to help.

Please, please carefully select facilitators of the committee's educational sessions. The worst mistake in the world (Stop! Think! Questionable claim fallacy; overstated!). Let me re-phrase that. It would be a mistake to announce to the committee an educational session that turns out not to be very educational.

Committee Chair: "OK, we're required by committee rules to start with a case discussion, so open your manuals to page…What? What's that? No, we don't have any extras. Looks like you brought yours, Harry. Open it to page 112, OK? Want to give the gist of that case or want me to?"

Then, following the impromptu case presentation:

"OK, anybody got anything to say about this case?" (Short Pause). "OK, let's call the meeting to order and get through this agenda and get outta here."

On Beyond This Primer and Practical Guidebook

Again, this guidebook neither attempts nor pretends to be an exhaustively complete compendium on health care ethics. Rather, the purpose of the guidebook is to serve as a starter resource.

For example, if committee members find the educational sessions helpful, each member could be asked to come up with additional cases for discussion, education, and practice.

Other traditional medical ethics issues include but are not limited to:

- *The professional ethic*. What is it and is it still alive and if not why not and should it be?
- *Informed consent*. Where do ethical aspects end and legal aspects begin? Or is there a clear demarcation line?

- *Protection of privacy*. Think privacy of personal medical information, physical privacy for hospitalized patients, and decisional privacy/autonomy.
- *AIDS*. What about mandatory testing? What about mandatory reporting? What about the ethics of caring for or refusing to care for an AIDS patient?
- *Organ Transplantation*. The ethics of harvesting; the ethics of recipient selection; the ethics of buying and selling body parts for transplantation purposes.
- *In vitro* fertilization, surrogate parenting and other traditional reproductive biology issues.

If you have suggestions about case topics to include in the second edition of this primer and practical guidebook, please send them to me at tmaret@sbcglobal.net.

Chapter 12

Living Wills and Surrogate Decision-Makers:
Voluntary Passive Euthanasia
The Birth of Hospital Ethics Committees

Case for Discussion

Charlene, a successful attorney and outdoorswoman, was diagnosed as having lung cancer when she was 52. Yes, she had been a cigarette smoker since age 14. After removal of one lung and a round of chemotherapy, Charlene resumed normal activities of daily living. However, three years later cancer was found in the other lung; metastatic lesions were also found in other organs. Cure was impossible.

Soon came the final hospitalization. Charlene was placed on a respirator. She remained fully conscious, communicating intelligently with family and friends by means of written notes. However, she was miserably uncomfortable. She was frustrated by not being able to talk because of the endotracheal tube. She knew that therapeutic remedies had been exhausted. She knew that she was simply waiting to die.

Charlene requested her physician, Dr. Barnes, to discontinue the respirator, aware that if he did, she would be dead within days if not hours. Charlene also wrote a note to her family members: "If you truly love me, let this happen."

Dr. Barnes consulted with the hospital ethics committee. After thorough questioning, the ethics committee recommended that Charlene's wish to die peacefully be granted.

Dr. Barnes wrote the order to discontinue life-support measures after giving Charlene a sedative, no stronger than one would take to get a good night's sleep. He also wrote a "Do not resuscitate" order. After giving Charlene the sedative, nurses and technicians pulled her endotracheal tube and removed all machines and medical paraphernalia from the private room to which she had been transferred. During this time, the hospital chaplain sat with Charlene's husband and parents, who were not religious and had no church affiliation.

With her husband and parents in attendance, Charlene died a peaceful death six hours after the respirator was removed.

Background Information

Many now think that autonomy, self-determination, is most often the ethical principle that trumps all others in situations involving withdrawal of life support or the decision not to start life-support measures in the first place. Some express this view as one kind of personal privacy, the privacy of decision making without external interference and/or judgments.

Others disagree, however. For some people, nonmaleficence is always the overriding consideration. Therefore, they might argue that removing the respirator caused harm because it allowed a preventable death. The common rejoinder to that argument might be an appeal to the principle of the difference between biologic life and high-quality human life.

An interesting aspect of this case is that Charlene was able to make her own decision. A much more common scenario is that an unexpected event, accident or serious illness has rendered a patient comatose or put them into a persistent vegetative state (PVS) before the person has a chance to make known his or her wishes in the event of an irreversible illness.

For this reason, the use of living wills, durable power of attorney for health care, and surrogate decision makers is common. In a living will, an individual states while healthy and mentally competent his or her wishes regarding life's end. The language of living wills must be exact, in the sense of compatible with and responsive to state laws regarding living wills and durable power of attorney. The ethics committee should ask hospital counsel or a knowledgeable hospital staff member to orient committee members to facts about living wills relevant to the statutes of your particular state.

In the absence of a living will (an occurrence becoming less and less common as awareness of them expands), a patient's doctors and nurses must rely upon care and treatment decisions made by someone designated to make choices for the irreversibly ill or irreversibly aged patient who is now comatose or in a PVS. This is not a good situation because bitter family battles often break out. In 2006, the sad case of Terri Schiavo became national news. Ms. Schiavo was in a persistent vegetative state. Her husband, Michael, claimed that Terri had asked not to be kept alive in such a condition. Terri's parents, devout Catholics, fought removal of life-support measures (a feeding tube) in court. Vote-hungry politicians became involved in this nasty scene. Eventually Ms. Schiavo's feeding tube was removed (in March 2006), and she died a peaceful death.

Enter the Ethics Committee

In 1976, in a famous ground-breaking case, the New Jersey Supreme Court upheld the request of a guardian to remove Karen Ann Quinlan's respirator and allow her to die. The respirator was removed, and Ms. Quinlan survived for ten more years, kept infection free with good care and prophylactic antibiotics and kept alive with M N&H (medically administered nutrition and hydration). During this time, ethical debates and court battles raged, regarding other cases, over whether or not a feeding tube (M N&H) is obligatory by moral considerations, or is not obligatory as in the case of a respirator? That issue is still debated today, but for the most part M N&H is considered to be a life-support measure and, as such, ethically and legally removable.

In the course of court proceedings in the Karen Ann Quinlan case, the court presumed that there was a deliberative and consultative body in each U.S. hospital to which a medical care team and a family could go for help and support when faced with such heart-wrenching ethical dilemmas. It was discovered that many hospitals had no such group or committee.

By the mid-1980s, hospital ethics committees were commonplace. Indeed, related requirements of the Joint Commission on Accreditation of Health Care Organizations helped stimulate the growth of ethics committees and appreciation of their important role.

Discussion Starter Questions

1. Name all of the stakeholders in this scenario. (*Stakeholders* is a jargon term used in ethics to indicate those individuals and/or groups whose interests are affected by decisions made and actions taken in a difficult situation (ethical dilemma).
2. How are the interests of each stakeholder affected by whether or not Charlene's request is honored and granted?
3. Who did something wrong (think incorrect and also think evil) in Charlene's case, if anyone? What did he or she or they do wrong, if anything?
4. In the 21st Century, what do you think this phrase means: "A fate worse than death?"

5. What questions would our ethics committee ask in this situation? Whom would we ask? Would we interview Dr. Barnes? Would we interview Charlene and/or her family members?
6. Legal aspects: Are members of the ethics committee at risk, legally—for example, might they be sued, or accused of murder—for recommending that Charlene's request to die be granted? If we don't know for sure, should we ask an ethicist, a doctor, a nurse, a health care executive, a minister, priest, rabbi or shaman, or should we ask an attorney knowledgeable about health care law?

Additional Resources

Tom Beauchamp and James Childress. *Principles of Biomedical Ethics, Fifth Edition*. Oxford and New York: Oxford University Press, 2001, pp. 120-8 and pp. 139-152.

Chapter 13

Assisted Self-Determination

Case for Discussion

Janet Adkins was a 54-year-old Oregonian grandmother with early Alzheimer's Disease. Janet was terrified of what she might become. She wanted her family to remember her as young and vibrant, not old and debilitated. This was a few years before assisted self-determination was made legal in Oregon.

(Note: Assisted self-determination, or voluntary active euthanasia, means honoring a person's request to provide the means whereby the person can end his or her own life. The term "assisted suicide" and the words "kill" and "killing" will be avoided, because they have no place in ethical debates about this issue. The reason is, in my view, those terms presume a conclusion. That defeats the purpose of ethical reasoning (Socratic discussion/debate), which is to discuss an issue in a detached manner, considering facts and logic before applying our moral values and emotions to the situation. The purpose is to avoid forcing our views and beliefs onto others. Note that the place for the words "kill" and "killing" and "suicide" is in the moralist's judgmental approach to the issue, condemning self-determination as against the Will of God as defined by the moralist. In addition, the words "kill" and "suicide" have standing in considerations of the legal aspects of this issue, because those words have meanings in the law that may or may not be the same as the meaning of the words in general usage, or in the context of a Socratic discussion/debate.)

On TV newscasts and in the newspaper, Janet saw stories about a Michigan pathologist who was a political activist, Dr. Jack Kevorkian. Dr. Kevorkian believes assisted self-determination should be legalized. In defiance of the law, Dr. Kevorkian rigged up a van with an apparatus that allowed him to start an IV in a patient's arm and then allowed the patient, by pushing a series of buttons, to administer a series of drugs, including a sedative and a heart-stopping overdose of potassium. Dr. Kevorkian offered his services to patients seeking assisted self-determination, which mainstream doctors and hospitals would have no part of.

Janet phoned Dr. Kevorkian. She flew to Michigan and met with him a few times over the span of one weekend. Then, Dr. Kevorkian drove her to a park in north Oakland County in his specially rigged van. He started an IV in Janet's arm with normal saline. Janet then pushed the buttons.

Background Information

Euthanasia literally means graceful death. Today, specifically, euthanasia means: The pre-planned ending of a human life to avoid the pain, suffering, and loss of dignity imposed by either terminal irreversible illness or the ravages of old age in a life exhausted of meaning.

Until recently, euthanasia was talked about only in hushed tones. However, this is now an openly debated subject because of 21st Century medicine's ability to extend biological life without necessarily extending meaningful human existence. Modern-day miracles can indeed make life for some a "fate worse than death."

The 2005 Best Picture Oscar went to *Million Dollar Baby*, directed by Clint Eastwood. The film's plot, to Mr. Eastwood's credit, acknowledges the reality that sometimes a health care professional or a family member with the means, in defiance of the law, honors a request to help someone escape a fate worse than death by ending life, now.

I hasten to acknowledge and do not want to offend the sensibilities of those whose religious beliefs preclude the euthanasia option under any circumstances. However, for those free to reason about this issue, here is some information relevant to discussion of the case presented above.

There are four types of euthanasia. (This is an arbitrary classification and is not the only one. This classification is simply a useful framework to help us organize our thoughts about euthanasia, and to understand the ethical impact of decisions made in a specific situation.)

Type 1: Voluntary or Non-voluntary Passive Euthanasia

(See Chapter 12). This is allowing nature to take its course by withholding ordinary and/or extraordinary treatment measures such as a feeding tube or a respirator or not starting such measures in the first place. This type of euthanasia is well-defined legally. Sudden catastrophic accident or illness can strike anyone at any time. The ethics committee should mount a campaign to encourage everyone of every age to have a living will specifying advance directives, known in some states as a Durable Power of Attorney for Health Care. Had Terri Schiavo executed such a document, her case probably would not have become infamous.

If life-support measures are withdrawn, or are not started in the first place, in response to a living will, life's end is voluntary and considered ethical and legal.

The ethics and legality of non-voluntary euthanasia (the patient is incompetent so a surrogate decision maker is responsible) depend on the facts in each case. Are the patient's best interests being served or is the surrogate decision maker serving his or her own interests? Often, as in the Schiavo case, this question must be answered by the courts.

Involuntary passive euthanasia would be pulling life-support systems against the patient's wishes, a very rare circumstance indeed.

Type 2: Assisted Self-Determination (Assisted Suicide)

The patient ends his or her own life, usually by injection, using a lethal substance provided by someone who has legal access to such drugs, such as a nurse or doctor.

Assisted self-determination is legal in Oregon. Slippery slope concerns expressed before this law was passed have not materialized. That is, criteria for obtaining assisted self-determination are clear and well monitored. People have not flocked to take advantage of the law, as some feared.

Type 3: Voluntary Active Euthanasia

The patient requests that someone, such as a trusted nurse, physician, relative, or friend, end his or her life by some means. Only painless euthanasia is ethical because of the nonmaleficence principle. This option would ordinarily require the availability of a lethal substance that can be injected into the patient by a willing health care professional. Voluntary active euthanasia is legal in Holland.

Objections to legalizing voluntary active euthanasia include concern for its impact on the image and practice of health care professionals. Would mixed signals be sent? "Well, you're not doing too well, Richard. There is an option I might mention."

"Quick, give me the names of three other physicians I can go to!"

Euthanasia activist Dr. Jack Kevorkian has ironically delayed serious consideration of legalizing voluntary active euthanasia in the United States for many years to come. Three times acquitted of criminal charges related to assisted self-determination cases, Dr. Kevorkian then crossed a line. In 1998 he arrogantly sent to CBS' 60 Minutes a videotape on which he is seen injecting a lethal substance into a patient at the patient's request. You can't videotape a murder and get away with it. If the courts had not convicted Dr. Kevorkian this time (keep in mind that the fact situation is different), might not respect for the law have been weakened? Dr. Kevorkian is currently serving a 10-25 year prison sentence for second-degree murder.

Type 4: Non-Voluntary Active Euthanasia

This is a mercy killing. Someone, ordinarily a nurse, family member, friend, or physician, decides euthanasia is the best choice and takes the patient's life. This is a legal issue. A mercy killing is murder or manslaughter, depending upon the facts.

Ethical Considerations

Note that, in considering ethical aspects of euthanasia, there are at least two important questions:

- Who decides that euthanasia is the best option? The patient or someone else?
- Who causes the patient's death? That is, does the patient die by his or her own hand, at the hand of another, or does nature take its course?

Euthanasia proponents list among possible beneficial effects:

- Reduction of suicide in the elderly because of new confidence that dignity and control of one's own life can be maintained all the way to life's end.
- A decrease in the incidence of sub rosa criminal active euthanasia by nurses and doctors in hospitals and nursing homes.

Opponents of euthanasia are informed either by religious directives, by slippery slope concerns, or by justifiable concerns about a person's ability to know when it is time to pick a day to die.

Discussion Starter Questions

1. Do we agree that there are four kinds of euthanasia? Or should all the forms of euthanasia be considered together when deciding whether or not euthanasia is ethical?
2. Who among us is best qualified to listen to and counsel a patient who is seriously considering assisted self-determination? If no one, what plans should we make now to get needed help if a patient and his or her health care team present us with this issue?

3. Do we agree that trigger words such as "killing" and "suicide" put a roadblock in the way of reason? Or does avoiding the words sidestep key issues that should be considered that can't be considered using any other words?
4. Ask each committee member: Do you have a living will? Have you ever wondered if you might someday choose assisted self-determination?
5. If we can euthanize our beloved old pets and "put them out of their misery," why can't we do it for humans? What's the difference?
6. Do we agree with the assumption that various circumstances in which euthanasia might be a choice should be treated differently, depending on which type of euthanasia?
7. If yes, does that mean we simultaneously think that assisted self-determination should be legalized? Should everything that is moral be legal and everything that is immoral be illegal?

Additional Resources

Tom Beauchamp and James Childress. *Principles of Biomedical Ethics, Fifth Edition*. Oxford and New York: Oxford University Press, 2001, pp. 120-8 and pp. 139-152.

Chapter 14

Purposeful Interruption of a Pregnancy

Case for Discussion

Marie, age 14, and John, age 16, are high school students. Both make good grades; they plan to go to the same college and get married sometime in the future. A week ago, Marie discovered that she was two months pregnant. Marie told John and her parents. John told his parents.

John plans to attend graduate school and wants Marie to have an abortion, because he wants to marry Marie but wants them to wait a few years before starting a family. John's parents agree and are willing to pay all her expenses.

Marie's parents are another story. Marie's mother was raised a Roman Catholic and has raised Marie a Roman Catholic; she does not want Marie to have an abortion. However, she does not want to give up her lifestyle to help care for a new grandbaby. Marie's mother suggests this solution: Have the baby and give the baby up for adoption. Marie's father, who is not religious, doesn't care one way or the other. He totally disowns both Marie and John for what he considers totally unacceptable, foolish, and immoral behavior.

Marie is very confused. Following her mother's suggestion, she has a counseling session with a priest who is sympathetic, yet tells Marie that she must not have an abortion because to do so would be a mortal sin. With the help of John's family, Marie has also discussed procedures and cost with a local abortion clinic staffed by reputable and competent physicians and nurses.

One of the physicians at the abortion clinic, also sympathetic with Marie's dilemma, suggests that she ask her own physician if the hospital's ethics committee would consider the situation and perhaps even talk to Marie. At this point, Marie has not yet decided whether to take that suggestion. Meanwhile, each day she grows closer to the end of the pregnancy's first trimester.

Background Information

The controversial question, "When does life begin?" is not the only factor to consider when deciding whether or not purposeful interruption of pregnancy is an ethical option in a specific difficult situation (ethical dilemma).

That statement and the following information only apply when religious directives do not dictate otherwise.

A utilitarian approach might anticipate the consequences of continuing the pregnancy. What would this mean for the mother? What opportunities might be lost? What would be the impact on the lives of individuals who must care for the child? Who is to say that these humanistic concerns should not be weighed against the unknown potential of the unborn child? Actually, many if not most would balance this pure ethical reasoning with a sense of moral value. Are adjustments of lifestyle not mere inconveniences when measured against human life?

A rights ethicist might point out that rights are not absolute. A major problem with rights ethics is deciding whose rights prevail in a given situation. Why should an unborn fetus have more rights than the biological mother?

Another problem with rights ethics is that this theory originally meant, "Be mindful of the rights of others." Today, for the most part, people are concerned with protecting their own rights. "I have a right to do this, so out of my way." In cases of interrupting pregnancy, defenders of mothers' rights and advocates for the unborn engage in vicious battles that are sometimes far removed from reasonable and civilized behavior.

Judith Jarvis Thomson makes a case for a woman's right to choose in an interesting way.[1] Suppose, writes Dr. Thomson, that in the middle of the night a woman is kidnapped and, against her will, connected with a variety of tubes to a famous violinist with end-stage renal disease. Without the hookup, the violinist will die within days. Is the woman obligated to preserve the hookup, or is she free to disconnect herself from this arrangement? Thomson argues that the woman is free to disconnect herself, because autonomy (self-determination) is an ethical value that often seems to trump other values. The woman did not agree to this arrangement, therefore, argues Thomson, she is free to terminate it.

Critics of Dr. Thomson's argument point out that it should be taken to apply primarily if not exclusively to rape cases.

A more common rights argument is at least implicitly based on the concept of potential. Should an adult woman with her life experience and potential have a right to build on and maximize that potential to the greatest extent possible? Most would answer, "Yes." However, what is the argument that this right should trump the right of an unborn fetus to be born? One answer is an argument by analogy. Which is a greater loss, some ask, the crushing of an acorn underfoot or the felling of a giant oak tree? Which trumps, being at the high point of a productive life or having unfilled potential? As in all ethical dilemmas, in most situations there is no answer that is either 100 percent right (correct, angelic) or 100 percent wrong (incorrect, evil).

Finally, the approach of some feminists seems ironic. On one hand, the right of self-determination is vigorously defended. On the other hand, some worry about logical extensions of this "right to privacy" argument. If everything done in one's personal life and one's home is to be free from legal intervention, some fear that this argument might at some time, in some circumstances, include abusive treatment of women and children. This argument might be far fetched in the context of practical ethics applied, or a slippery slope argument without foundation. Nevertheless, the argument is one that is included for logical completeness in the deliberations of theoretical ethicists.

Awareness of a variety of valid viewpoints regarding this and other difficult issues can help us understand, and therefore develop a better working relationship with, those who hold views different from our own.

Discussion Starter Questions

1. Who are the stakeholders in this situation? List them all.
2. What role does each stakeholder play in deciding what Marie does? Who provides input? Who makes the final decision? Who should/must be informed of the decision?
3. Would your ethics committee consider a request such as the one suggested by the sympathetic abortion clinic doctor? If so, why, since Marie is not a hospitalized patient? If not, why not?
4. If your committee encountered a situation similar to the above, what would you suggest be the committee's recommendation(s)? On what ethical theories, ethical principles, and/or moral guidelines do you rely in making this recommendation (these recommendations)?

5. With respect to this and other issues, who keeps the ethics committee advised of any relevant religious directives, state and federal statutes, regulations, and judicial precedents that affect the work of an ethics committee?

Reference

Judith Jarvis Thompson. "A Defense of Abortion." *Philosophy & Public Affairs*. 1(1): 47-66, Fall 1971.

Part VI

Issues and Cases for Discussion:
Organizational Ethics Applied to Health Care

Chapter 15

A Hospital and Executive Staff Define "Reasonable Self-Interest"

Case for Discussion

At the Annual Board and Executive Staff Planning Retreat, the CEO (Chief Executive Officer), CFO (Chief Financial Officer), and Board Chair propose that the governing board approve a definition of reasonable and acceptable profit.

Why? Who suggested that this be on the retreat agenda? And who suggested that specific wording, "reasonable and acceptable profit?" Was it the hospital's ethics committee? Good heavens, isn't the definition of profit tacitly understood? Isn't the goal to make as much money as possible? Isn't that just a given? Isn't that what being in business means? Shouldn't that just go without saying (meaning, without thinking about it)?

Maybe, but in this case the agenda item comes from the marketing department. In executive staff meetings, the Marketing and Advertising VP keeps suggesting that, "People are so sick of dishonest businesses that a visible show of admittedly old-fashioned and nearly obsolete caring concern might sell really well. Besides, we need to show people that we really do know the difference between reasonable profit and greed."

Other senior executives, including the CEO but excluding the CFO, plus the board chair and several board members who were asked to comment on this idea, decided that sure enough, a reputation for keeping care in managed care spread through the community by word of mouth might be more effective than even a five- or six-figure formal marketing campaign.

At this moment in the planning retreat, the whole group gets caught up in this idea. The notion of "reasonable self-interest reflected in a definition of reasonable profit" ceases to be a mere agenda item. The moment becomes a happening. Indeed, as often happens in retreats, this moment sets a theme and tone and provides a unifying buzz phrase (reasonable self-interest) that turns a mere planning retreat into a memorable experience.

Now to add the details. How shall the newly awakened and aware board and executive group define "reasonable profit?" A month later, at the next board meeting, a report on the planning retreat includes a request to approve the budgeting guide for the coming year—a definition of reasonable profit inspired by the happening at the retreat.

The board approves the following definition of reasonable profit:

"This year's profit goal shall be 30% of revenue. In an effort to achieve this goal, money-losing services such as the high-risk nursery, the emergency services area, and indigent clinics used by our university-related teaching programs will be closed, if at all possible without generating bad public press and/or legal difficulties.

"In addition, downsizing and outsourcing efforts will be intensified, going far beyond what is necessary to maintain our designation as a Top 10 Hospital.

"Because of our new guideline, reasonable self-interest, an additional 0.5% of revenue will be used to supplement budgets of hospital departments providing direct patient care services, instead of being invested in the market to achieve higher profit for investors.

"A clarification: This definition of reasonable self-interest and reasonable profit shall be implemented in such a way that it does not affect either executive salaries or expansion plans.

"The Marketing Department is instructed to prepare a press release advising local newspapers and TV newsrooms of our compassionate caring and concern."

In the retreat's next to last session, inspired by its own magnanimity, the board/executive group unanimously adopts revisions in the language of the hospital's Mission Statement and Code of Ethics, promising more and greater compassion and high-quality care.

Background Information

Some people who really want to act ethically just don't know how. The baggage they carry gets in the way. Who can blame a group of highly successful business-trained individuals for remaining true to what they believe is expected of them—safeguard finances and, in a profit-taking organization, maximize profit?

Is the board really being unethical, or is it just missing the mark in terms of achieving the impact desired by the marketing department?

The board/executive group in the above story does act ethically, because one ethical school of thought is utilitarianism. The utilitarian equation requires that actions be chosen that produce the greatest net good. This is often misquoted as "the greatest good for the greatest number." That is usually the case, but sometimes to achieve great good for a small number, a larger number of people might suffer only inconvenience. This, too, fulfills the utilitarian equation.

Even if a board member is guided in his or her professional life by a Divine Command ethic, he or she might in good conscience vote for the definition of reasonable profit that the group arrived at. Because, the person might truly feel that God has placed him or her in a position to be on the board for just such a moment—to be sure that the board fulfills its fiduciary responsibility, which means (in non-legal terms) keeping the hospital from going broke. Of course, in that case, someone might remind this board member of a board's other fiduciary (ultimate) responsibility, which is the safety and effectiveness of services provided. At some point, downsizing the nursing staff does not exactly contribute to patient safety, does it?

The point is: If we do not know what considerations drive a person's stated views and in this case, vote, on an important matter, and if those views and votes do not coincide with our own, we tend to think of ourselves as ethical and moral and the other person as unethical and immoral. This is what self-righteous means.

Discussion Starter Questions

1. In the above scenario for discussion, the hospital's ethics committee had no input. Should the Ethics Committee, or representative members, have been asked to participate in this matter, or at least been asked to prepare a guidance statement to be read to the retreat group?
2. If our Ethics Committee were asked to provide such a guidance statement, how would we respond?
3. What definition of "reasonable profit" does our ethics committee suggest?
4. Health care is, in one sense, a critical social service. Are the concepts of social service and profit compatible?
5. Does this case scenario for discussion have any relationship to state and federal health care policy? If so, what? If not, why not?

Chapter 16

Integrity in Advertising

Case for Discussion

A few years ago, as part of a presentation on ethical and legal issues, I warned a group of board members, executives, and physician leaders that advertisements can be perceived as promises. "If I understand my attorney friends correctly," I said, "an ad creates a promise and people can get sued for not keeping such a promise."

In the afterglow of the meeting, as I talked with the hospital CEO, the President of the Medical Staff, a highly respected internist, joined us. Shaking his head, the doctor said to the CEO: "Darn it, Will, I told you we should have actually bought the new laser and credentialed a doctor to use it *before* we ran that ad!"

Background Information

Integrity means honesty. Keeping promises is part of being honest.

Advertising and marketing are not synonyms. Marketing is a multifaceted endeavor involving everything from conceiving and producing a new product to servicing and selling the product. Advertising is announcing to the public that a product is available. Effective advertising also creates the image that everybody needs one of these, whatever the new product is. In the ad, information about the product accentuates the positive and eliminates the negative.

There is no such thing as a 100% honest truth teller. We all tell little white lies. Little white lies are the meat and potatoes of advertising. Indeed, the very business of advertising is to praise the product while at the same time whispering negatives or speaking the fine print really fast.

"World's Biggest Hamburger!" *where "world" is the two blocks of Main Street between 2nd and 3rd Avenues*. We don't care that advertisers do this. We know to expect it. We find that example funny. However, we would stop laughing if the hamburgers we got were not average size or above, fresh, and tasty. We would be especially upset if the hamburger ad seriously deceived us and our life truly depended on that hamburger!

Too much deceitful advertising can create a consumer expectations gap. That is, high consumer expectations created by the ad are not met by the company's production department. The result can be loss of public trust in the company and its products.

In addition to the ethical principle of truth telling, advertising relates directly to Kantian deontology, duty/obligation based ethics. One example of Kantian ethics usually given is keeping promises. Misleading ads test this ethical principle, too.

Some ads are truly honest and effective marketing, designed to sell the product by presenting the product honestly. The company delivers what it promises. Effective ads focus on the positives in one's own product rather than denigrating the product(s) of a competitor.

On the other hand, deceptive and misleading ads have only one purpose—take the money and run, leaving the complaint department and the legal department to handle the fallout.

Truth telling and integrity are two of the most used, most respected ethical principles in creation. A company's ads compared to experience with the company's products tell any critically thinking citizen a great deal about that company's genuine commitment to providing high-quality, dependable merchandise at affordable prices. That public perception can affect market share positively or negatively, depending on the nature of the ethic that guides the company's advertising policies.

Discussion Starter Questions

1. Is keeping promises created in advertising purely a legal and public relations issue, or are there ethical aspects to this issue as well? If so, what are the ethical aspects? That is, what ethical theories and/or ethical principles and/or moral values apply?
2. Should a double standard be applied to health care advertising vs. other companies' ads? That is, should the health care business be held to a higher truth telling and promise keeping standard than other businesses? If so, why? If not, why not?
3. Review your hospital's ads. Do any of them deceive the public? If yes, in what way? Is the deception outside acceptable limits of misleading people or lying outright in an advertisement?
4. If the answer to question 3 is "Yes," does the charge of your ethics committee include calling this public impact to the attention of the marketing department? Or is advertising none of the ethics committee's business?

5. Do professionals who advertise, such as doctors and lawyers, sacrifice at least some of their traditionally respected professional standing by advertising like any other profit-seeking business? If so, how? If not, why not?
6. Should there be a working relationship between a hospital's marketing/advertising department and that hospital's ethics committee? If so, what should that relationship be? If not, why not?
7. Is attention to ethical advertising likely to decrease profit? If so, why? If not, why not?

Part VII

Case Studies for Discussion:
Medical Bioethics

Chapter 17

Pre-Gestational Genetic Diagnosis

Case for Discussion

Molly Nash and her little brother, Adam, are school-age children living in Englewood, Colorado. Molly, the oldest, was born with Fanconi's Anemia (FA). FA is a genetically transmitted (inherited) disease ordinarily causing death in childhood. The only known treatment for FA is a bone marrow transplant from a genetically matched individual who does not have FA. (If the donor is not genetically matched, the transplant recipient might reject the transplant.) Such a donor could not be found.

Mr. and Mrs. Nash went to a special *in vitro* fertilization clinic in Minneapolis that specializes in pre-implantation genetic diagnosis (PGD). There, eggs were harvested from Mrs. Nash and impregnated *in vitro* with sperm from Mr. Nash. The resulting embryos were tested for the presence of the FA gene (this is PGD). An embryo genetically identical to Molly except with no FA gene was selected and implanted into Mrs. Nash's uterus. Nine months later (August 29, 2000), Adam Nash was born, a child created for the purpose of being a bone marrow donor for his sister.

Almost immediately Molly received a transfusion of Adam's cord blood, which contained many stem cells capable of producing normal red blood cells. The treatment worked. Molly is fine, and so is Adam.

Lisa and Jack Nash, Molly's and Adam's parents, were totally surprised that their situation became famous. They have never allowed either Molly or Adam to be interviewed, and it is said that they will not talk to anyone who seems eager to get into an ethical discussion.

Background Information

Amazing technological advances in artificial reproductive biology and genetics disturb and challenge long-held, deep-seated notions about the creation of human beings and the meaning of life. Indeed, use of the word "artificial" defines the problem in these areas. There is nothing artificial about a person created by IVF (*in vitro* fertilization), yet it seems natural to some to speak of IVF as artificial, as unnatural.

Some of these issues are household words because they are political footballs. For example, development of needed treatments using stem cells requires research, and design of those research studies must include use of human stem cells. The stem cell itself is not an issue. A cell that has the potential to grow into either a bone or a heart or a nerve is part of nature. There could be no complex human beings, no scientists intelligent enough to be pioneers in these vast new frontiers, if it were not for the potential of stem cells.

The issue, rather, is one rich source of stem cells, the human embryo. In natural reproduction, a diploid zygote is formed by the union of a man's sperm with a woman's egg, which are special haploid cells known as gametes. After a few cell divisions, this product of fertilization, whether *in utero* or *in vitro*, is known as an embryo. That embryo is considered a citizen with human rights by some; others believe that it becomes impractical to try to equate acorns with oak trees.

In IVF, many embryos are created, but only one is implanted into the uterus of a woman to become a newborn then a child then eventually an adult. The other embryos can be frozen for later use—raising, by the way, the issue of ownership of the embryos in case of divorce—or they can be discarded.

In embryonic stem cell research, an issue that hopefully will soon be obsolete because of advances in understanding stem cells from more acceptable sources, one issue is the belief of some that discarding a human embryo is the equivalent of premeditated murder.

Flying under the radar (so far) is another relatively new technique that involves discarding unused artificially created embryos. PGD, pre-gestational genetic diagnosis, is now offered in several locations around the country. PGD means testing embryos in several ways to determine characteristics that will be of interest if the embryo becomes a human being.

Keep in mind: When you hear the word, *embryo*, don't think of a partially developed human curled up inside a mother's uterus, with a long umbilical cord. That is a *fetus*, a later stage of development. Remember, an embryo is only a few cell divisions removed from the formation of a zygote by the union of two gametes. Don't worry about the medical jargon. Suffice it to say, an embryo is a clump of cells whether the embryo is *in utero* or in a petri dish.

The obvious purpose of PGD is to leave nothing to chance in terms of getting the kind of child parents want. Now that you are conditioned to think like an ethicist, and are capable of doing so, the ethical aspects of this situation are immediately obvious to you, aren't they.

To begin with, what about the Kantian exhortation that if civilized society is to remain civilized, human worth must be the primary consideration? Individuals must not be used as a means to an end. Is not Adam being used? Of course he is, because there would have been no Adam Nash if there had been no need to find a bone marrow or cord blood donor for Molly. There might have been a brother for Molly, and that brother might have been named Adam, but he would not have been the same individual created under these circumstances.

By the way, if Adam were a product of natural fertilization occurring as a result of sexual intercourse, the embryo from which he grew would be indistinguishable from an embryo created by *in vitro* fertilization (IVF).

Speaking of creating Adam, does this sort of practice change the very nature of creation? Does this capability knock into a cocked hat the old notion that only God can make a person? Some say no. The starting point was a naturally occurring egg and a naturally occurring sperm. Thus, they might argue, it is a mistake to speak of Adam as being man-made.

Nonsense, say others. Is Adam not a living, breathing, human being, a student in elementary school? Yes, he is. And did he not emerge from the artificial, unnatural process employed by the scientists whom the Nashes employed? Yes, he did. Then most certainly Adam was created by mortal men and women, and not by God.

Note that try as we may to be logical and objective when engaging in ethical reasoning, ethical arguments almost always in the end rely upon what we choose to believe. Indeed, please keep in mind the admonition that ethical reasoning not balanced with moral values seems an empty academic exercise.

What about Adam's autonomy, his right to self-determination? Once he has served his purpose, once Adam's cord blood has been harvested and transfused into Molly, who needs Adam anymore? What is to happen to him? Is he to have a life of his own?

By the way, as you are probably thinking, this is entirely up to what kind of parents the Nashes are. To all outward appearances, Adam and Molly are equally nurtured and equally cherished by their parents. Indeed, many familiar with this story agree that in this case, Adam's autonomy is well-served because of the Nashes commitment to both Adam and Molly.

From the perspective of another ethical principle, where's the justice? Should PGD be available only to those willing and able to pay for it? The Nashes presumably went to considerable expense to seek out the clinic in Minnesota, travel there, and pay costs of this procedure and the ensuing pregnancy and delivery. Does justice require that in health care, what is available to one is available to all? Some would say that this issue, and others such as disposition of unused human embryos, is not unique to PGD. Indeed, this line of thinking might lead us into matters of economic and social justice, and we might end up talking about national health care policy and the uninsured.

Are there ethical objections that relate specifically to PGD? Some say, yes, there are.

What if parents use PGD in a situation that does not involve medical therapy? Is it ethical to use PGD to balance a family? What if parents have three girls and want another child but specifically want a boy and specifically do not want another girl? Is it ethical to use PGD as an earlier technique of pre-natal sex selection, which has been an issue ever since it has been possible to know the sex of a fetus with some certainty?

With respect to human cloning and PGD and other issues, where does reasonable concern about potential future events end and madman fantasizing begin? What if some brilliant but warped scientist funded by some demon who wants to take over the world decides to populate the world with one kind of individual? Is it ethical to create a master race?

More in the realm of possibility, what if parents want to select an embryo that is male and has genetic characteristics suggesting the potential to be athletic and have a chance at someday landing a big bucks professional sports contract? What if a mother wants a designer baby, with the potential to grow into a famous, highly paid model? Those who have dealt with ambitious parents (I am a former pediatrician) will not lightly dismiss such "yes but, what if…?" scenarios.

Ideally, practitioners in clinics and institutions offering PGD accept if not welcome guidance from a relevant institutional ethics committee. What sorts of questions should those ethics committees ask, do you suppose?

Discussion Starter Questions

1. Should our health care facility/facilities offer PGD? If so, why? If not, why not?

2. If PGD is offered, should practitioners be asked to follow guidelines about acceptable and unacceptable indications for using PGD?

3. Who in our institutions, organizational leadership, and/or community is knowledgeable about PGD? If no one, if this is an issue for us, where can we get more information?

4. By the way, let's don't forget to ask: Are any of our obstetricians and clinical geneticists offering PGD?

5. Do directions regarding moral values of the organization and its health care facilities take this decision out of our hands? For example, is there language in our Ethics Code or Mission Statement relevant to this issue? Are some of these questions answered for us by relevant religious directives?

6. Should we be politically active in this area? In the halls of state and federal government, does PGD deserve more attention or does stem cell research deserve less? Or is that question any of this ethics committee's business?

Some Resources

http://www.emedicine.com/med/topic3520.htm

http://plato.stanford.edu/entries/parenthood/

Chapter 18

Nanotechnology

Case for Discussion

The year is 2027. Barbara Belmont has life-threatening bacterial sepsis (infection of the blood stream) and purulent abscesses in several organs. The causative germ is staphylococcus aureus, so-called because laboratory colonies of staph aureus are a golden yellow color.

In the pre-antibiotic era no treatment was effective for this condition. Now (in 2027), it is the post-antibiotic era. Overuse of antibiotics for several decades gave almost all known bacteria a wonderful opportunity to develop resistant strains. Developing resistance is a natural adaptive capability that involves evolutionary changes in a bacterial cell's metabolic processes.

For example: penicillin once killed staph aureus by interfering with synthesis of its all important protective cell wall, without which a staph cell is as vulnerable as we would be without our skin. Today, in 2027, tiny metabolic factories inside each staph cell merely ignore penicillin, having over the years developed an alternate assembly line for making cell walls.

No matter. Today, in 2027, the treatment of choice for bacterial infections is no longer antibiotics. There is a new way to disrupt a bacterium's intracellular metabolic mechanisms. It is the age of Nanomedicine.

Doctors introduce into Barbara's body billions of tiny nanorobots, sub-atom size particles designed to enter bacterial cells on a search and destroy mission, much like a Pac man-like computer game. The nanorobots disrupt, confuse, interfere with, and eventually annihilate each staphylococcal cell's tiny metabolic factory.

These nanorobots or nanoparticles are themselves products of other nanorobots known as replicators They are designed and manufactured to visit their devastating blows only to staph cells.

Barbara's temperature drops from 105 degrees Fahrenheit to a normal 98.6. Using techniques that have remained essentially the same for two centuries, Barbara's abscesses are surgically drained.

Within a few days, Barbara recovers. She is discharged home and resumes her usual activities of daily living. Her life is restored to normal. Normal, that is, except for the existence in her blood stream and vital organs of billions of tiny foreign nanorobots.

Background Information

Nanomedicine is one application of nanotechnology. A nanometer is one billionth of a meter; that is, about one billionth the length of a yardstick. Complex chemicophysical, subatomic size particles inside the cells of nature's basic building blocks measure 100 nanometers or less. Nanotechnology is a combination of chemistry and engineering, a new science that works with these nanoparticles.

Within a few decades, tiny nanomachines, thousands of which would fit into the period at the end of this sentence, may be able to construct hard goods at the molecular level, again revolutionizing industry. Famine could be eradicated by fabricating foods using nanotechnology.

Nanomedicine applications include treating cancer and infectious disease, understanding and influencing the aging process, enhancing human intelligence, and sending tiny nanorobot surgeons into a person's body to operate without producing scars.

Nanotechnology, including nanomedicine, is not yet a reality. At the same time, it is not totally science fiction. In 2000, President Bill Clinton requested $227 million to fund a National Nanotechnology Initiative. The NIH (National Institutes of Health) has established eight Nanomedicine Development Centers, centerpieces of the NIH Nanomedicine Roadmap Initiative.[1] Researchers have successfully tested in mice a nanocell system that delivers chemotherapeutic agents to a cancerous site in the mouse's body, and DNA nanoparticles have been used to accomplish gene transfer in patients/research subjects with cystic fibrosis.[2]

Ethicists agree that nanotechnology, including nanomedicine, raises many troublesome issues. Nanoparticles might be engineered that, introduced into the human body, provide information about us that is useful for medical purposes. Any practicing physician will tell you that it would be wonderful to develop a diagnostic system of direct observation, instead of having to rely on one unreliable historian (patient) after another. However, might this capability not require a whole new definition of "the right to privacy."

Are there limits within which human enhancement is acceptable? What if tiny nanofactories are put to work re-engineering our bodies to resist various diseases, but also to enhance human cognitive functions and/or muscular strength? Does the term "master race" then rear its ugly head?

If we discover that we can arrest the aging process at some point, should we?

Where's the social and economic justice? What causes for the common good will have to go underfunded if funding for nanotechnology becomes a high priority?

Though ethicists generally agree that such concerns must be addressed, starting now, they disagree about how to address them. Some say a brand new ethics will have to be developed—new schools of thought, new ethical principles, new moral values—to deal with nanotechnology. Other ethicists say, "What's new?" The Hastings Center, a leading bioethics think tank, sees challenges to "values we have long embraced…autonomy, beneficence, fairness, efficiency, and environmental preservation."[3]

The French Centre National de la Recherché Scientifique[4] recommends an eight-part plan for dealing with ethical aspects of nanoscience and nanotechnology, including nanomedicine. The eight-part plan includes (paraphrased):

1. Conduct forums for discussion, gatherings of representatives from manufacturing companies, consumer associations, patients' associations, and government to consider ethical aspects of nanotechnology.

2. Include awareness of and education about ethical aspects in training/education of research workers.

3. Produce short ethics guides for research scientists.

4. In research facilities, set up ethics forums for internal discussions of ethical aspects related to current projects. Scientists, engineers, and technicians should exchange views and share interests with individuals working in the humanities and social sciences.

5. Increase awareness of and stimulate interest in nanotechnology in the humanistic and social science community.

6. Establish mechanisms for detecting and arbitrating conflicts of interest between nanotech scientific projects and industry. As part of this effort, ensure transparency of the source of funding of nanotechnology research projects.

7. Educate the public about expected benefits of nanoscience and nanotechnology, including nanomedicine, without hiding the fact that possible harm can result from applications of nanoscience. Dare to consider even fantasies to which nanoscience might give rise.

8. Establish permanent groups for dialogue/debate at the local, national, and international level.

As with other scientific matters in recent years, a similar set of clear guidelines does not exist in the United States. In the United States, today's version of democracy demands that we be position-takers, vigorously defending our rights to embrace or reject new scientific developments, as opposed to problem-solvers engaging together in reasonable discussion/debate about them.

What does the emergence of nanomedicine mean for U.S. hospitals, physicians and medical education, nurses and other currently indispensable health care professionals, patients and the community of potential patients and taxpayers, insurance companies, institutional providers, and the hospital ethics committee? No one knows.

One thing is clear, however. The future always starts now. That is, the future usually depends on the nature and direction of first steps taken along paths either carefully chosen or forced upon us by our own decisions and actions. Ignoring abuses of nanomedicine could be another nail in the coffin of the Socratic and Aristotelian notion that with careful thought and determined will, it is indeed possible to keep society civilized.

Discussion Starter Questions

1. Should the ethics committee be aware of and learn more about nanomedicine, or is this matter too futuristic to warrant attention at this time?

2. Should the ethics committee be politically active? Should the committee recommend to the hospital's executives and board a stance for or against encouraging research in nanotechnology in the United States?

3. And, don't forget to ask: Are any of our doctors or other staff members especially interested in, knowledgeable about, or even active in nanotechnology research?

4. Is anyone in our community a potential nanoethics resource for the ethics committee?

References

1. www.nihroadmap.nih.gov, The NIH Nanomedicine Roadmap Initiative.
2. Paul Litton. "Nanoethics? What's New?" *Hastings Center Report* 37(1):22-5, January/February 2007.
3. *Ibid.*, p. 23.
4. www.cnrs.fr

Printed in the United States
74594LV00002B/1-150

9 780978 730604